Writing for Advanced Learners of English

FRANÇOISE GRELLET

CAMBRIDGE
UNIVERSITY PRESS

To Charles

THANKS

I am very grateful to Dominique Chevallier, Kathleen Haddon and Charles Kaye for their help and encouragement. I also wish to thank Ruth Brown for her valuable suggestions, and Lindsay White at Cambridge University Press for her constant support and advice.

ACKNOWLEDGEMENTS

The author and publishers are grateful to the authors, publishers and others who have given permission for the use of copyright material. While every endeavour has been made, it has not been possible to identify the sources of all material used and in such cases the publishers would welcome information from copyright sources. Apologies are expressed for any omissions.

P1: from *Four Quartets* © 1943 by TS Eliot, renewed 1971 by Esme Valerie Eliot, repr by perm of Faber and Faber Ltd and Harcourt Brace & Co. P2-3: from *Laughing Matter* K Batchelor (ed), pub by Topaz Records/Accelerated Learning Systems Ltd. P4: repr by perm of Hellas, National Tourist Organisation of Greece. P5: © the *Observer* 1992. P6: from *The Dead of Jericho* by Colin Dexter, pub by Macmillan General Books. P6-8 letters: from *Pick of Punch* repr by perm of *Punch*. P9: sentences from Ruth Rendell, *Kissing the Gunner's Daughter*, repr by perm of Peters Fraser and Dunlop Group Ltd, pub by Hutchinson/Arrow. P10: 'the european community' from an article by Allen Hamilton in *The Times* © Times Newspapers Ltd; from *Love and Friendship* by Alison Lurie, © Alison Bishop 1962, pub by William Heinemann Ltd and repr by perm of Reed Consumer Books Ltd and Aitken, Stone & Wylie Ltd. P11: 'Pupils do it in stone' by Maggie Parhams ©*The Times* 20 Dec 1995. P13: © the *Independent* 1 Sept 1993; 'It's your life' taken from an advertisement by Motorola Ltd. P14: © *The Times* 28 Aug 1993. P15: advertisement © *The Times* ; also p17 'Psychiatrist reverses famous face' by Jeremy Lawrance, 14 Dec 1992. P18-19: from 'A Time To Die' by Aileen Wheeler, repr in *New Tales of the Unexpected*, pub by Penguin Books Ltd. P20-2 : from the story 'Taste' taken from the volume *Someone Like You* by Roald Dahl, © 1959 by Roald Dahl; pub by Michael Joseph and Penguin in the UK/Commonwealth and repr here by perm of Murray Pollinger. Pub by Alfred A Knopf Inc in the USA and Canada. Originally appeared as a story in *The New Yorker*. P22-3: from the story 'The Landlady' in the volume *Kiss, Kiss* by Roald Dahl, pub by Michael Joseph (1961) and Penguin in the UK/Commonwealth and repr here by perm of Murray Pollinger. Pub by Alfred A Knopf Inc in the USA/Canada. P24: from *Summer's Lease* by John Mortimer, pub by Penguin © Advanpress 1988. P25: from Maurice Baring, *Lost Diaries and Dead Letters* pub by Alan Sutton Publishing Ltd. P27: 'Little Johnny's Final Letter' in *Notes to the Hurrying Man* by Brian Patten, pub by HarperCollins Publishers Ltd. P28-9: three passages from *Put on by Cunning* by Ruth Rendell pub by Hutchinson/Arrow and Co and repr by perm of Peters Fraser and Dunlop Ltd. P30: 'Culture shocks' by Terry Murphy from the *Independent* © 26 Oct 1993. P31: Ionicus cartoon repr by perm of *Punch*. P33: 'Benjamin Franklin's Sister' repr by perm of Charles Kaye. P35: 'Handle with passion' repr by perm of Toyota (GB) Ltd; 'Pressed for time' repr by perm of Sunbeam-Oster International Ltd; 'Let Barclays' repr by perm of Barclays Bank PLC; 'Defy the Joneses' repr by perm of Nissan Motor Corp USA; 'We put a lot of energy' repr by perm of Rayovac Corp; 'Fashioned by aerospace' repr by perm of Saab Great Britain Ltd. P36: Basho haiku from *Matsuo Basho* by Makoto Ueda, pub by Kodansha International Ltd © 1982 by Kodansha International Ltd. Repr by perm. All rights reserved. Carol Stuart haiku from *The Forms of Poetry* by Abbs and Richardson, pub by Cambridge University Press. P38: Part XII of 'Fragments from the Japanese' from *Primrose Path* © Ogden Nash, by perm of Little, Brown and Company and Curtis Brown Ltd; and 'There were once two people of taste' from *A Choice of Comic and Curious Verse* JM Cohen (ed), pub by Allen Lane and Penguin. P41: from 'Eight Riddles from Symphosius' in *Advice to a Prophet and Other Poems* © 1961, renewed 1989 by Richard Wilbur, repr by perm of Harcourt Brace; pub in the Commonwealth by Faber in *New and Collected Poems* by Richard Wilbur. 'Riddle-me-Ree' by Liz Lochhead from *Dreaming Frankenstein* and *Collected Poems*, pub by Polygon Books (Edinburgh University Press). P42: from

CONTENTS

TO THE STUDENT

The aim of this book is to encourage you to write and take pleasure in writing. The focus is not on language and grammar but on activities that will lead you to free expression.

The different units therefore progress from simple activities to more complex ones, from guided writing to free expression.

Throughout the book you are encouraged to do the various writing tasks individually, then to evaluate, analyse and revise your draft through pair work or discussion with the whole group. The individual work is essential to apply the rules or advice you have been given as well as to become independent and overcome your possible 'fear of the blank page'. But the group work is just as necessary: most pieces of writing are meant to be read by someone else and the reactions of others are a good test of the clarity and effectiveness of what you have written. The comments of your fellow students should also help you edit and improve your work and thus develop the critical mind essential to a writer.

TO THE TEACHER
AIMS

1   This book is for advanced students of writing who already have a good command of English grammar and vocabulary and have had practice in writing a range of everyday text types (e.g. letters, postcards, newspaper articles). The material provides a wide range of challenging activities that will develop students' imaginative and creative writing skills.

   It can be used as the core of an advanced writing course or as supplementary material to complement another course and give more emphasis to writing. It can be used with students attending general English courses in universities, language schools or secondary schools.

2   Students are encouraged to study and experiment with a large variety of text types (e.g. stories, poems, articles, book reviews, limericks, advertisements, riddles) as well as writing procedures (e.g. editing, correcting, imitating, parodying). It is true that students will probably never need to write poems or advertisements 'in real life' and that these tasks are not likely to be required for specific exams. But such activities, besides motivating students and developing their appreciation of text types, are language awareness exercises that lead them to think about words, rhythm, and the best way of conveying an idea clearly and concisely. They are therefore formative as well as rewarding.

   The book will also sensitize students to aspects of writing such as punctuation, bias, point of view, style and implied reader, which are as essential to reading as to writing. Indeed, most of the units start from reading material and lead students from analysis to production.

The book thus aims to give students the opportunity of trying more inventive or creative forms of writing and to help them become more critical of their own and others' writing. This dual approach is designed to enable students to enjoy fully the process of writing.

STRUCTURE OF THE BOOK

PART A

Manipulation focuses on some aspects of accuracy in writing: improving and editing texts, punctuation, selection of important information, different text types and their rules of composition. For example, students are invited to:

- rewrite and edit poorly written texts;
- shorten and lengthen texts;
- suggest words to complete texts;
- transform one text type into another (e.g. an extract from a novel into a newspaper article).

PART B

Imitation brings together activities in which students can be as inventive as they wish within a given framework such as a particular genre or writer's style. Activities in this part include for example:

- writing in a variety of genres (e.g. acrostics, advertisements, proverbs);
- parody and pastiche.

PART C

Variations on a theme leads students to explore parallel but different ways of expressing ideas. They are, for instance, asked to:

- write articles or accounts in a biased or unbiased way;
- tell a given story from different points of view;
- write stories or essays, observing particular stylistic constraints (e.g. without any adjectives, or without any relative clauses).

PART D

Invention contains more open writing activities. For instance:

- finishing a poem or a story;
- writing about pictures.

METHODOLOGY

1   This book is a sourcebook rather than a coursebook. Even though the overall progression from PART A (*Manipulation*) to PART D (*Invention*) is from guided writing tasks to more open-ended ones, there is no strict sequence to follow. For instance, the unit on bias in PART C might well be used before that on parody in PART B, if it is needed to reinforce something else that has been studied in class. The book should therefore be used in a flexible way, according to students' needs and interests.

2   Since most units move from reading to analysis, and then from controlled to freer writing, it is important to respect the order of the tasks within each unit. However, a number of similar activities are often suggested at the end of each unit which do not all need to be completed. Some can be given as homework, or kept for further practice or revision later in the year.

3   The units are meant to be used flexibly and there is no ideal lesson length. Some can be covered in 45 minutes, others will require two or three hours, depending on the level and motivation of the class as well as on the number of tasks chosen.

4   The approach is largely through group work, in which a text or concept is discussed, followed by individual or pair work for writing, followed once more by group work for discussion and feedback. While personal writing is essential, student interaction and peer evaluation will help to stimulate discussion, to develop students' critical abilities, and to get them to see their fellow students as potential 'critical readers', whose responses to a piece of writing may reflect its communicative value (e.g. its clarity, persuasiveness, emotional impact).

5   Because many of the activities are open ones, it is impossible to predict the structures and vocabulary students will need for a given activity and so to prepare the ground beforehand with systematic lexical and syntactic practice. This means that this more formal approach to language, which is essential, will probably have to take place afterwards, through revision or practice of language points which students have had difficulty with. The feedback on written work should therefore come:

   – from the students' discussions and sharing of their work;
   – from the teacher, whenever he or she provides individual correction of the student's work;
   – from the teacher, who, at regular intervals, will focus the attention of the class on aspects of language where they need improvement.

6   The open-ended nature of the activities has also meant that it has not always been possible to provide a model or suggested answers. But the Key at the end of the book provides possible answers for a number of activities.

And every phrase
And sentence that is right (where every word is at home,
Taking its place to support the others,
The word neither diffident nor ostentatious,
An easy commerce of the old and the new,
The common word exact without vulgarity,
The formal word precise but not pedantic,
The complete consort dancing together)
Every phrase and every sentence is an end and a beginning …

(From T. S. Eliot, 'Little Gidding')

In this section, you are asked to work on existing texts rather than create new ones. You will have to rewrite or edit passages, expand or contract others, finish incomplete texts or transform one type of text into another. The aim here is to help you focus on accuracy as well as on text types and their rules of composition. Such activities will therefore show that the form of the text is as important as its contents.

A.1 Developing a critical mind

All writers need to check and recheck what they have written. They are rarely content with their first draft and feel the need to read it over in order to improve it. This critical phase of any writing job is very much what editors do when they read manuscripts or articles. Editing a text requires a certain distance and you may find it easier to leave aside the text you have just written and wait for a few hours before looking at it again with a critical eye.

A.1.1 Rewriting

1 The following sentences or paragraphs from newspapers are all genuine. But they are so poorly written that the passages have become comic, absurd or meaningless, which is why they have been reprinted in an anthology of British humour.

Read the passages and:

- find out why the sentences are comic or absurd;
- rewrite them as you would if you were the editor of the newspaper.

a
BEDFORD FIREMEN today received 28 letters thanking them for their efforts which destroyed 3 houses last Wednesday night.

(Bedford paper)

b
BODIES IN THE GARDEN ARE A PLANT SAYS WIFE

(*Hong Kong Standard*)

c
The driver had a narrow escape as a broken board penetrated his cabin and just missed his head. This had to be removed before he could be released.

(Leicester paper)

d
THE RETIRING police commissioner has been responsible for all crimes committed in the district for the past twenty years.

(*Wembley (V.A.) News*)

e

> Now retired, he lives with his wife, a beautiful blonde and a San Francisco girl.

(*Ansonia (N.H.) Graphic*)

f

Spotted man wanted for questioning

(*Hackney Gazette*)

g

> Dying is to cost more at King's Lynn, Norfolk. Higher burial charges are being introduced at cemeteries. The increased cost of living is blamed.

(*Daily Telegraph*)

(From K. Batchelor (ed.), *Laughing Matter*)

Now compare your 'corrected' versions with the others written in your group. Have the original ambiguities been eliminated?

2 The following excerpts from letters of request for money or help are obviously so badly written that the messages have become absurd.

Working in pairs or small groups, decide who the writer is, and to whom he is writing. Then rewrite the letters so that the meaning becomes clear.

a *I want money as quick as you can send it. I have been in bed with the doctor for a week and he doesn't seem to be doing any good. If things don't improve I shall have to send for another doctor.*

b *Milk is needed for the baby and Father is unable to supply it.*

c *Sir, I am forwarding my marriage certificate and two children, one of which is a mistake as you will see.*

d *Please send some money as I have fallen into errors with my landlord.*

(*ibid.*)

Exchange your rewritten versions of these passages. Can you notice any remaining ambiguity or shift in meaning in the new versions?

A.1.2 Editing

1 The two passages that follow are part of an advertisement for Macedonia. Look at the first one and study the corrections that have been made. Then correct the second passage in the same way.

Aristotle

Aristotle, the tutor of Alexander the Great, was born in Stagira in Macedonia, in 384 BC. Together with Plato, he is regarded as one of the greatest philosophers the world knew. Aristotle was a true academic, concerned for Physics, Astronomy, Rhetoric, Literature, Political Science and History. His teachings had laid the foundation for modern scientific thought.

/has known
/with
/have

Alexander the Great

Alexander was born in 356 BC in Pella Macedonia established by his father, Philip II, as the centre of the Hellenism. Nurtured on the thoughts of his tutor, Aristotle, he rose to fame like brilliant military leader. He influenced the corse of history rightfuly earning his title as Alexander the great. In 335 BC he becomes Military Chief of all the Greeks. By the time of his death in 323 BC he created an enormous empire, stretching from Adriatic Sea to the Indias, and from Caucasian Moiuntains to Egypt. He spread the greek spirit far and wide among nation who idolise this great man.

(Correct version from Hellas, National Tourist Organisation of Greece, London)

What sort of errors were you able to identify? Spelling? Punctuation? Vocabulary? Grammar?

Compare your corrected versions. Are they similar? Discuss any differences between them.

2 The draft of an article about Cleopatra's Needle is given below. Edit the article, which contains a good many errors. Look for:

one relative pronoun mistake
four article mistakes
two spelling mistakes
four capital letter mistakes

three punctuation mistakes
three tense mistakes
three preposition mistakes
one agreement mistake

Egypt Seeks Return of Ancient Obelisk

EGYPT wants Cleopatra's Needle back. The Egyptian embassy claims the ancient obelisk, a London landmark, would be better cared for in Cairo than ecposed to traffic fumes of the Embankment.

'Cleopatra's Needle should be in a museum in Cairo. In London it faces enviromental hazards,' said the embassy's cultural councillor Hussein Sayed.

The embassy's call follow a campaign by egyptian experts that are angry that so much of their heritage is abroad 'We would like to see the return of important objects in museums in Egypt, said professor Abdul Halim Nureldin, Vice-Dean of Cairo University and former director of the government's Antiquities Organisation.

Cleopatra's Needle has had a chequered history. Dating of 1500 BC, it was one of a pair of obelisks carved for Pharaoh Thutmose III and erected at Heliopolis, near modern Cairo. Augustus Caesar has moved the two obelisks at Alexandria in 12 BC. Although now known as Cleopatra's Needles, there is no historical basis to the romantic story linking them to Egyptian Queen.

Britain was given one of the obelisks in 1819 by the Viceroy Mohammed Ali an Albanian who ruled Egypt for the Turks. The gift was to thank Lord Nelson for defeating the french and restoring Turkish control.

Cleopatra's Needle has long toppled over and was lying abandoned in the sand. The task of shipping 186-tonne pillar was daunting and it was not until 1877 that a cylindrical iron vessel is built to transport it to London.

(Correct version from the *Observer*, 5 April 1992)

Compare your edited articles. Have you all found the same mistakes?

3 Edit the following letter so as to make it correct and clear.

Dear Mister Richards

Its about Missis Scott who died, I now all about you and her but does Missis Richards. I now ALL about it, I hope you beleive me because if you dont I am going to tell her everything, You dont want that. I am not going to tell her if you agree, You are rich and what is a thousand pounds. If you agree I will not bother to rite again., I keep all promises beleive that. The police dont now anything and I have never said what I now. Here is what you do, You go down to Walton Street in Jericho and turn left into walton Well Road and then strate on over the little Canal brige and then over the railway brige and you come to a parking area where you cant gomuch further, then turn round and face Port Medow and you will see a row of willow trees, the fifth from the left has got a big hole in it about five feet from the ground. So put the money there and drive away, I will be watching all the time. I will give you a ring soon and that will be only once. I hope you will not try anything funny. Please remember your wife.

(From Colin Dexter, *The Dead of Jericho*)

Compare and discuss your edited versions.

4 The following series of four letters appeared in *Punch*. Read the letters and try to imagine what James will do after he receives Mr Baggs's answer.

Yooth Wanted

To Messrs. Plugg and Gaskett, Ltd, Motor Engineers
DEAR MR. PLUGG AND GASKETT – I see by your advert that you require a junior Clerk that is quick at figures. You say you woold prefere one just left School, well I have just left School so pheraps I woold do? I was 3rd in my class for Maths and Top for Algabra, but pheraps you woold not re-quire any Algabra? I was farely good at most subkjects exept English grammer and competition, so pheraps you will let me know? I am very intrested in Motor Enginering and I am sure you woold find me just right for the job.

Yours truly,

J. HOOP

To Mr. G. R. Hoop

DEAR UNCLE GOERGE, – I am writing to ask if you woold do me a favuor as Dad says you might. The thing is, I have been trying to get a job in a office now that I have left School and have answered twelve adverts in the paper but dont get any replys, and I think it is proberly becuase I dont know how to write business letters. Dad says as you are a buisness man and better educated than the rest of the famly pheraps you coold helpme, wich I woold be gratefull if you woold Uncle as I am at my wit's end and dont want to become a buchers boy or anything like that. I hope you are well.
Your afectionate nephew,

JAMES

To Messrs. S. Baggs and Son, Coal Merchants

SIRS, – With reference to your advertisement for a junior clerk in The Evening Bray of to-day's date, I beg to be considered for the post.
I am a youth of 15 years and, until recently, attended the Central Modern School, where I stood high in most subjects. I was particularly proficient in Arithmetic.
I may add that I am extremely interested in the coal distribuitive trade and am not without some association with it since my uncle, Mr. G.R. Hoop, is Transport Manager to Messrs. Waites and Scales, Ltd., of Shovelham.
I enclose a copy of my late headmaster's testimonial, which will, I think, give you confidence in my suitability for the post.

I am, Sirs,
Yours respectfully,
J. Hoop

To Mr. J. Hoop

DEAR MARSTER HOOP, – It seams by yore leter you are just the sort of chap wear looking for, tho I ort to exsplane that my litle biznes is not a big consern like the one yore Uncle works for. But now that wear doing a bit more trade we cood do with sumbody to look arfter the books proper. Most of all we needs sumbody as can write proper biznes leters, and by the looks of yore one to me you wood do fine. Drop round enny time.

Yores truely,
SAM BAGGS
C. E. DAVIS

(From *Pick of Punch*)

Pick out some of the mistakes, then rewrite the first, the second or the fourth letter, correcting the spelling and grammatical mistakes and making it sound more natural.

Then compare and discuss your corrected versions of the letters.

A.1.3 Punctuating

The role of punctuation is to make the text you write clear and easy to read. Defective punctuation can make a text very difficult to understand, and even lead to misunderstandings.

Compare, for instance, the following two sentences and explain how the change in punctuation brings about a change in meaning:

    a The theory he explained was very impressive.
    b The theory, he explained, was very impressive.

Then rewrite the sentences to make their meaning clear without relying on the use of commas.

  ☞ *1* Explain how the change in punctuation creates differences in the meanings of the pairs of sentences that follow.

    a (i) His nephew, who works for IBM, is a friend of Sheila's.
        (ii) His nephew who works for IBM is a friend of Sheila's.
    b (i) Thinking he would know, I asked the MP who had just been elected.
        (ii) Thinking he would know, I asked the MP, who had just been elected.

c (i)   He invited those who were reluctant to leave.
   (ii) He invited those who were reluctant, to leave.
d (i)   Surprisingly, excited as she was, she gave the right answers.
   (ii) Surprisingly excited as she was, she gave the right answers.
e (i)   It was a large party and John had brought his two sisters, Anne, and Christine.
   (ii) It was a large party and John had brought his two sisters, Anne and Christine.
f (i)   The members, who had not been warned, were furious.
   (ii) The members who had not been warned were furious.
g (i)   The director, said Brian, had come up with a brilliant idea.
   (ii) The director said Brian had come up with a brilliant idea.
h (i)   Everyone knew, he thought, that she would resign.
   (ii) Everyone knew he thought that she would resign.

2 Punctuate the following sentences.

a the gun was among a jumble of textbooks dog-eared exercise books crumpled paper and a pair of football socks and for a single frightening moment martin thought it was real

b he had come out early not only to take his son to school that was incidental a by-product of leaving the house at ten to nine but to have a new pair of windscreen wipers fitted to his car

c his credit card would not be needed here to back the cheque for everyone knew him this was where he had his account he had already caught the eye of one of the cashiers and said good morning

d the man who had the gun in his hand said in his flat nasal tones nothing will happen to you if you do as you're told

e martin shouted get back call the police now there's been a robbery

(From Ruth Rendell, *Kissing the Gunner's Daughter*)

Then compare and discuss the sentences you have punctuated.

3 Here are two passages without any punctuation. Punctuate them, using the guidelines you are given.

Passage 1. Add the following punctuation:

ten capital letters
two full stops
six commas
one colon
one dash
one set of inverted commas

> the european community was a success story as was evident from the number of applicants waiting to join in a speech reflecting last friday's birmingham summit the queen said the british presidency is working to build on that success developing a community of all 12 member states which draws on the strength of each which meets the needs of their people listens to their anxieties and responds to their wishes a community which is open to the rest of europe and to the world

(From *The Times*)

Compare your new versions of the article. Are they all similar?

Passage 2. Add the following punctuation:

twenty-nine capital letters
twelve full stops
ten commas
nine sets of inverted commas
six question marks
four dashes linking five words to form an expression
two colons
one semi-colon
two words in italics

> at the top of the hill will pulled to the side and turned off the engine there you are he said through the windscreen emmy saw layers of interlocking snow-covered hills receding one after another ...
>   well will said he smiled at emmy but made no move she tried to think of something to say hunting nervously about in her mind and managed
>   Breughel ... it's like the hunters in the snow with all the houses and people taken away
>   will made no comment finally he said tell me about your parents you like them don't you
>   yes i do really she heard herself answer
>   what are they like very old family and keeping up the stockwell traditions
>   oh no you've got quite the wrong idea the stockwells aren't anything really really nouveau riche

(From Alison Lurie, *Love and Friendship*)

Compare the punctuated texts within your group. Are there any differences? If so, discuss them.

Now look at the punctuation of the original passages on page 128. See in what way it differs from yours.

4 Here is another article to punctuate if you would like further practice.

Pupils Do It In Stone

half a century after the engraver letterer and sculptor eric gill died his spirit and philosophy live on through his last pupil david kindersley

this week apprentices from kindersley's cambridge workshop are perched on scaffolding above euston road adding the ring of the hammers and chisels to the whine of London traffic as they cut the words the british library in enormous roman capitals from blocks of red scottish sandstone

kindersley now 77 bearded and with a long balding head not unlike gill's wraps the proceedings in rich wafts of cigar smoke as he talks about his mentor

he says gill believed in making things that people wanted he used to talk about this art nonsense and ask what's it all blooming well for most especially he was totally at variance with the teaching of art in art schools …

like gill kindersley insists that his apprentices come to him free of artistic training he points to the letterers ranged along the scaffolding cornelia arrived from holland on a bicycle she had been a teacher but felt she needed to make things with her hands guy used to be a civil servant owen has just left high school in yukon

---

(From *The Times*, 20 October 1992)

A.2 Expanding and contracting

In the activities that follow you are given texts that are written in good, correct English but whose length has to be increased or reduced. The length of a text is an element you often have to take into consideration when you are writing: you may be assigned the task of writing an essay, abstract or article of a specific length; or a newspaper editor may have to fit a 'latest news' item into a given space; or again certain types of texts (e.g. small ads) cost more or less depending on the number of words or lines they contain.

Length is therefore an important factor, and changing the length of a text will oblige you to think about which words, sentences or ideas are essential and which are secondary.

A.2.1 Expanding

1 Divide into groups and read the following article.

> ## Post-op office
>
> AN NHS HOSPITAL is offering rooms with telephones and fax machines so patients can continue working after operations. Standish Hospital in Stonehouse, Glos, will even provide secretaries.

In each group, one person should suggest an addition to the article, of no more than eight words. The addition can be a single word (e.g. *efficient* secretaries) or a whole sentence (e.g. *The cost will be £200 a day*), but there should be only one point of insertion. The other people in the group note down the addition, and then someone else suggests his or her own way of expanding the article. The activity goes on until each person has contributed two additions. Clearly you will be adding information but these additions should not change the overall meaning of the article.

When you have finished, check your new article and then compare and discuss the versions produced in each group.

2 Choose one of the following articles and, working individually, add an extra 30 words to it (either whole sentences or isolated words or phrases) without changing the main idea of the article.

Built to last

A 92-year-old Johnson motorcycle owned by Scunthorpe Museum Services, Humberside, passed an MoT with its original brakes, tyres and steering.

(From the *Independent*
1 September 1993)

Bias claim settled

Susan Sadjady, 29, of Northolt, west London, accepted £2,000 compensation from the Territorial Army for sexual discrimination after being rejected for an interview as a trainee paratrooper and being told she might be suitable to do some cooking.

(From the *Independent,*
1 September 1993)

Then compare and discuss the new versions of each article produced in your group.

1.2.2 Contracting

1 Here is the text of an advertisement for a mobile telephone.

It's your life. Motorola will help you live it the way you want. As the world's largest mobile telephone manufacturer we've developed the technology you need to put you in control.

Now we make telephones small enough to take across international boundaries and still stay in touch if you want to.

So you can be where you want to be, do what you want to do, call who you want to call.

That's the kind of choice you have when you choose a Motorola phone.

For more information call 0500 555 555.

1 Reduce the text by fifteen words without rewriting it. What words would you delete?
2 Now choose a slogan for the mobile telephone. It should have no more than twelve words and should already be contained in the advertisement.
3 Compare and discuss the advertisements and slogans suggested in your group.

2 You are told that for editorial reasons you need to cut 30 words from the following article. You are not allowed to rewrite the article. What words or sentences would you delete?

Bank raider caught by his ears

A BANK robber was jailed for ten and a half years yesterday after being identified by his ear "print". Bobby Lee Clarke, 24, of Shoreditch, east London, wore a mask when he raided Barclays Bank in Aveley, Essex. He was filmed by security cameras inside the bank and his exposed ears and eyebrows were singled out as vital clues in his conviction.

Police used a computer at the new Facial Identification Centre, based at the Charing Cross and Westminster Medical School, Hammersmith, west London, to compare the bank photographs with others of the suspect. Clarke was arrested two months after the raid. Dr Peter Venezis, who heads the centre, told the jury at Snaresbrook Crown Court that human ears were like fingerprints, with no two the same.

"The contours of the ear match in both images," he said.

Clarke was arrested driving one of two stolen cars used in the robbery. A sawn-off shotgun and ammunition were found in the vehicle. The jury took a little over an hour to find Clarke guilty of robbery, two counts of unlawful possession of firearms, firing a firearm with intent to endanger life and reckless driving.

(From *The Times*, 28 August 1993)

Then compare and discuss the decisions taken in your group. Can your group's ideas help you to improve your version?

3 Most small ads use abbreviations in order to save space. Read the following ads and write down what the abbreviated words stand for.

a
> **NW6** – Queens Pk, prof m/f, n/s, own lge rm, shr hse nr tube, £70 per week 0171......

b
> **WIMBLEDON** Immac 2 bed hse in priv mews. Patio/gdn, priv pkg, v. close BR/tube. £180 pw. Call 01372......

c
> **CLAPHAM STH** Immac 2 dble bed hse. Lux f/f kit. inc d/w, w/m. Lge bath. Sunny gdn. £200 pw. 0171......

4 You have already run the following ad in a local paper but haven't sold your house yet. You decide to place another ad in *The Times*, but cannot afford more than three lines. Fill in the form below. You will have to rewrite your ad, using abbreviations whenever possible and keeping only the essential information.

> **ASHFORD MIDDLESEX.** One bedroom ground floor maisonette. Situated in private road, easy reach of town & all major routes. Large lounge, kitchen, bathroom & double bedroom. Small front & rear gardens. Garage at rear £82,500. Tel: 0174......

Write your advertisement below (approximately 28 characters per line including spaces and punctuation). Minimum 3 lines. £5.50 per line plus VAT, or £8.25 per line plus VAT for 2 weeks.

NAME

ADDRESS

TEL (Day)   SIGNATURE

If you would like to take advantage of our dual insertion plan, and **save 25%** please tick box. ☐
No advertisement can be accepted under these special terms unless pre-paid.
Cheques should be made payable to Times Newspapers limited or debit my:

ACCESS ☐   VISA ☐   AMEX ☐   DINERS ☐   (Tick box)

Card No.

This offer is open to private advertisers only. Trade advertisers will appear subject to the normal rates and conditions.   Exp Date

Send to: Simon Goddard, Advertisement Manager, The Times, Times Newspaper Ltd, PO Box 484, Virginia Street, London E1 9BL.

TELEPHONE 0171 481 4000   FAX 0171 481 9313 or 782 7828

Compare the new ads written in your group. Did you keep the same information?

5 A friend of yours has gone to Italy and asked you to forward any important letters or messages poste restante, in a number of cities. You send her a telegram which must contain the following information:

Summerfield College is considering her for a job which is just what she has always dreamed of. She must ring them and arrange an interview no later than next Friday. Their telephone number is 0171 899 5400.

Can you write the telegram in no more than ten words?

Compare the different telegrams written in your group. Which are the clearest ones? Why?

6 Here is an article on Leonardo da Vinci's *Mona Lisa* and a 115-word summary of it.

KEY TO MONA LISA'S SMILE MAY BE IN LEONARDO'S MIRROR

By Jeremy Laurance

Psychiatrist reverses famous face to reveal artist's secret

THE enigma of the Mona Lisa's smile, a subject of dispute for centuries, may have a simple explanation. The face of the unknown sitter, famous for its strangely sinister quality, may be a mirror image of Leonardo himself, according to a psychiatrist in London.

The sinister aspect to the smile, described by Sigmund Freud as expressing the contrast between "the most devoted tenderness and a sensuality that is ruthlessly demanding," arises because of the way we "read" faces with the two halves of our brain, says Dr Digby Quested, a registrar at London's Maudsley hospital.

The Mona Lisa smiles more with the left side of her face, which is normally true of forced smiles and is more common in men. Reversing the portrait gives the face a warmer, more appealing aspect.

"The face looks as though it is the wrong way round," Dr Quested said yesterday. "The key to its mystery is that it is a mirror image."

Leonardo was known to be left handed and produced mirror writing, so could have created the inversion unintentionally. But Dr Quested suggests in the Bulletin of the Royal College of Psychiatrists that the painting is more likely to be a self-portrait.

"There was evidence that he was homosexual and he may have felt trapped in his sexuality," he said. "It may be that people saw him as one thing but he felt he was another and didn't feel free to express it. Painting himself as a female would have helped him."

The theory that the Mona Lisa is a portrait of the artist enjoyed brief attention in the mid-1980s, when a computer-aided juxtaposition of her face with an acknowledged self-portrait of Da Vinci showed that the facial features aligned exactly. Dr Quested cites other evidence to support the theory, however. Mystery surrounds the identity of the sitter and the commissioner of her portrait. Leonardo was "almost certainly infatuated" with the picture, keeping it with him until his death in Paris. Leonardo's tutor, Andrea del Verrocchio, cast a statue of David for which the young Leonardo was thought to be the model, whose half-smile bears a striking resemblance to Mona Lisa's. X-rays of the painting have revealed a bearded face.

"I believe Da Vinci worked it out," Dr Quested said. "He may have shown the finished face to others who commented on the strangeness of the smile and he tried to work out why this was so. Being left handed and producing mirror writing, he must have been interested in the idea that the two halves of a face can convey different messages."

"The painting is a self-portrait in inversion, both with regard to laterality and gender."

(From *The Times*, 14 December 1992)

Summary

A London psychiatrist believes that the face of the Mona Lisa, with its enigmatic smile, might be a mirror image of Leonardo himself. The Mona Lisa smiles more with the left side of her face, something usually true of men and of forced smiles. Dr Digby Quested concludes that the painting must be a mirror image, possibly a self-portrait of Leonardo. As a homosexual, Leonardo may have wished to escape his sexuality by painting himself as a female. This would also explain why the identity of the sitter is unknown and why Leonardo was so infatuated with the portrait. 'The painting is a self-portrait in inversion, both with regard to laterality and gender,' he says.

1 Reduce the summary to 80 words.

2 Use the article to help you to expand the summary to 150 words.

A.3 Completing

In the activities which follow you are asked to complete texts from which some parts have been omitted. These activities are of course partly comprehension exercises since the context largely determines the kind of words or sentences which you can use. But there still remains a range of possibilities for each blank space, and the choices you will have to make will force you to compare and contrast the relative value of different words and phrases – an activity which is at the heart of writing.

1 Here is the beginning of a short story from which all adjectives have been omitted. Fill the blanks with adjectives which you find appropriate in the context.

Ellison Liddell was a ……… man and inordinately ……… of his

handiwork.

    Born into a ……… family of ……… parentage, he had soon shaken off

his ……… origins and by ……… deployment of his ……… abilities in the

field of electronics, his ……… talent, capacity for ……… work and ………

---

ruthlessness in the removal of all obstacles, he had, in his ……… forties, acquired very ……… business interests, a ………, ………, exquisitely ……… house, ……… cars, holiday properties overseas and not one ……… cloud in his ……… sky. Most men in his position would have been ……… to rest upon their laurels. Not so Ellison.

He had enjoyed accumulating his wealth; now he aspired to two more of life's ……… prizes – an honour of some sort and an heir. The stumbling-block to both these ambitions lay in the person of his wife, Dulcie.

Recently, he had spent much time painstakingly cultivating the ……… people and, although normally ……… with money, had begun giving largely to ……… causes, pretending dismay when the news of his ……… generosity was carefully leaked.

Unfortunately, Dulcie did not share his ……… aspirations, proving, in fact, a ……… embarrassment to them, so, with the ……… efficiency that characterized all his enterprises, he decided to dispose of her, completely and soon. She was too ………, anyway, to provide him with the son he so desired and now that he had met Violette, a ………, ……… French woman, widow of a ……… business competitor, he knew he had found the ……… partner. Wealthy in her own right, she possessed the looks, breeding and business acumen that made her infinitely ……… in his eyes. What a hostess she would make! What a ……… mother of his children! He sensed also, correctly, that she was equally attracted to him, for he had retained his ……… good looks and was not without a ……… ……… charm. Only ………, ……… ……… Dulcie stood between him and the ……… marriage. Dulcie was a drag. Dulcie must go.

(From Aileen Wheeler, *A Time to Die*)

When you have completed the text, compare and discuss the different versions produced in your group. Are there some adjectives which you think are in contradiction with the meaning of the text? Do others, on the contrary, open up

A.3

interesting possibilities as to what may happen in the rest of the story?

You can, if you wish, produce a collective version of the text by selecting the adjectives you prefer from those proposed in your group.

You can then compare your version with the original text on pages 129-30.

🔑 2 The passage that follows is the end of a short story by Roald Dahl, but you are only given the narrative parts. Can you write the missing dialogue? It should be easier if you read all the narrative passages first in order to understand what the story is about.

(*Richard Pratt, a famous gourmet, has been invited to dinner at his friend Mike Schofield's house, and has bet him that he will be able to tell him the name and vintage of the wine served at dinner. The stakes are extremely high. At this point, Mike has fetched the wine which had been left to 'breathe' in the study and has filled Richard's glass. Richard has taken a couple of sips of the wine.*)

[Richard Pratt] hesitated, and we waited, watching his face. Everyone, even Mike's wife, was watching him now. I heard the maid put down the dish of vegetables on the sideboard behind me, gently, so as not to disturb the silence.

    '.........' he cried. '...'

For the last time, he sipped the wine. Then, still holding the glass up near his mouth, he turned to Mike and he smiled, a slow, silky smile, and he said, '..'

    Mike sat tight, not moving.

    '...............................'

We all looked at Mike, waiting for him to turn the bottle around in its basket and show the label. ...

    '................' his wife called sharply from the other end of the table.

    '................................?' '...'

Richard Pratt was looking at Mike, smiling with his mouth, his eyes small and bright. Mike was not looking at anyone.

    '.........' the daughter cried, agonized. '......................................
............................'

'…………………………,' Mike said. '…………………………'

I think it was more to get away from his family than anything else that Mike then turned to Richard Pratt and said, '…………………………
…………………………………'

'…………………………,' Pratt said. '…………………………'

He knew he was a winner now; he had the bearing, the quiet arrogance of a winner, and I could see that he was prepared to become thoroughly nasty if there was any trouble. '…………………………' he said to Mike. '…………………………'

Then this happened: the maid, the tiny, erect figure of the maid in her white-and-black uniform, was standing beside Richard Pratt, holding something out in her hand. '…………………………,' she said.

Pratt glanced around, saw the pair of thin horn-rimmed spectacles that she held out to him, and for a moment he hesitated. '…………………………
…………………………'

(…) Without thanking her, Pratt took them up and slipped them into his top pocket, behind the white handkerchief.

But the maid didn't go away. She remained standing beside and slightly behind Richard Pratt, and there was something so unusual in her manner and in the way she stood there, small, motionless and erect, that I for one found myself watching her with a sudden apprehension. Her old grey face had a frosty, determined look, the lips were compressed, the little chin was out, and the hands were clasped together tight before her. The curious cap on her head and the flash of white down the front of her uniform made her seem like some tiny, ruffled, white-breasted bird.

'…………………………,' she said. '…………………………
…………………………'

It took a few moments for the full meaning of her words to penetrate, and in the silence that followed I became aware of Mike and how he was slowly drawing himself up in his chair, and the colour coming to his face, and the eyes opening wide, and the curl of the mouth, and the dangerous little patch of whiteness beginning to spread around the area of the nostrils.

'.......................,' his wife said. '...'

(From Roald Dahl, *Taste*)

When everyone has completed their stories, compare your different dialogues in groups of five, if possible. Are they all based on the same plot? How would you describe each dialogue? Is it, for example, realistic, amusing or full of suspense? Or all three? You can then, if you wish, compare your dialogue with that of the original text on pages 130–31.

You may want to act out one of the dialogues written by someone in your group. Each person can play the part of one of the five characters (Richard, Mike, Mike's wife, the maid, the daughter).

3 This time you are given a passage from which the descriptive prose has been omitted. Can you fill the blanks, choosing one of the following possibilities:

– The dialogue is part of the realistic description of the scene
– The dialogue is part of a macabre story, or of a thriller
– Other.

Read the whole passage and the title given below before attempting to fill in the blanks.

(*The narrator, who has been looking for a hotel, has just seen a 'Bed and breakfast' sign outside a house.*)

....

....

'*Please* come in,'..

....

....

'I saw the notice in the window,' ....

'Yes, I know.'

'I was wondering about a room.'

'It's *all* ready for you, my dear,'..

....

'I was on my way to The Bell and Dragon,' ....'But the notice in your window just happened to catch my eye.'

'My dear boy,' ...., 'why don't you come in out of the cold?'

'How much do you charge?'

'Five and sixpence a night, including breakfast.'

....

'If that's too much,' ...., 'then perhaps I can reduce it just a tiny bit. Do you desire an egg for breakfast? Eggs are expensive at the moment. It would be sixpence less without the egg.'

'Five and sixpence is fine,' .... 'I should like very much to stay here.'

'I knew you would. Do come in.'

....

....

....

'Just hang it there,' she said, 'and let me help you with your coat.'

....

....

'We have it *all* to ourselves,' ....

....

A.3

(From Roald Dahl, *The Landlady*)

When you have finished, compare and discuss the different stories written in your group. Can you identify the style of each of them?

A.4 Transforming

In the activities that follow, you are asked to transfer the information contained in one text type to another.

This is in fact quite a common type of activity: when something important or interesting happens in our lives, we often describe it in various forms of written English. If, for instance, your bag or wallet has been stolen, you may mention or refer to the incident in:

- a telegram or fax to your family asking for money;
- a letter to the local newspaper to complain about thieves;
- your diary;
- a letter or postcard written to a friend;
- a message left to a friend to explain why you can't meet him or her.

These activities will be useful as a reminder of the variety of text types you can use and of their rules of composition. They will also encourage you to think about the register of the text you write, that is to say its degree of formality. In a letter to a friend, you will probably use colloquial English, whereas a letter of complaint or another type of official letter will have to be written in a more formal way.

🔑 *1* 1 Read the following instructions which appear in the novel *Summer's Lease* by John Mortimer. They have been left by the owners of a villa to the family who are renting it for the holidays.

> The villa 'La Felicita' can only be enjoyed by the observance of strict rules and a certain discipline. Most of these rules will be obvious. The wasteful use of the bathrooms, for instance, can turn a summer holiday into a time of intense anxiety and the purchase of water by the lorry load may strain the budget of even the best-heeled family. None of the following devices should, on any account, be switched on at the same time: the immersion heater in the master bathroom, the swimming-pool filter or the dishwashing machine. If a hair-drier is in use, it's generally wise to temporarily disconnect the refrigerator. More detailed instructions will be found taped on the walls over the appliances concerned. Above all, avoid flushing the lavatory next to the small sitting-room more than once in any given half hour or serious results may follow.

These instructions are not expressed by means of imperatives. What structures are used?

2 Rewrite the instructions in a more direct and concise way, using imperatives. Then, in groups, compare and discuss the different sets of instructions.

2 Here is an imaginary letter written by Odysseus to Penelope[1].

THE ISLAND OF OGYGIA

Dearest Penelope,

We arrived here after a very tiresome voyage. I will not tire you with the details, which are numerous and technical. The net result is that the local physician says I cannot proceed with my journey until I am thoroughly rested. This spot is pleasant, but the only society I have is that of poor dear Calypso. She means well and is most hospitable, but you can imagine how vexed I am by this delay and the intolerable tedium of this enforced repose. Kiss Telemachus from me.

Your loving husband,
Odysseus

(From Maurice Baring, *Lost Diaries and Dead Letters*)

Write the telegram or the postcard Odysseus might have sent Penelope instead of writing a letter.

Then compare the different telegrams or postcards written in your group. Which information did you consider important enough to retain?

[1]Odysseus (or Ulysses) was king of the Greek island of Ithaca. After distinguishing himself during the Trojan war, he embarked on his return voyage but met with numerous adventures (related in Homer's *Odyssey*) and only reached Ithaca, where his wife Penelope was still waiting for him, twenty years later. Calypso was the queen of Ogygia. She kept Ulysses there for seven years.

3 Look at the notes which accompany the two advertisements below. The two people who wrote the notes obviously went to Egypt or ordered a clearblind, but are not satisfied. Using the information you are given, draft a letter by one of these two people. Draft (a) a letter of complaint or (b) a letter to a friend describing their holiday or new purchase.

A.4

ANCIENT EGYPT

Enjoy both the fascination of Ancient Egypt and the luxury of first-class hotel accommodation on one of our week-long holidays in Luxor. Our itinerary includes all the major sites and still leaves you with plenty of free time. Most days begin with sightseeing trips, and leave you free in the afternoon to relax by the pool or go browsing in the colourful shops.

only had two free afternoons

Direct flights from Gatwick to Luxor mean that you can start your holiday straight away without the usual overnight stop in Cairo.

The hotel we use is in a glorious position on the banks of the Nile with magnificent views of the West Bank. All rooms are air-conditioned and have private bathrooms. Hotel facilities include swimming pools, bars, restaurants, shops and gardens.

OK

During your stay you will have the chance to:
● go to Karnak Temple – in a horse-drawn carriage *tour bus instead*
● cross the Nile to the West Bank to see the Valley of the Kings, the Valley of the Queens, the Tombs of the Nobles, the Temple of Hatshepsut at Deir el Bahari, Medinet Habu, the Ramesseum, and the Colossi of Memnon *no time to go* *two of these were closed for restoration*
● visit Luxor Temple
● go down-river to the temples at Edfu and Komombo.

8 DAYS FROM £350.00

Departure dates & prices

(per person twin room – Mondays from Gatwick)

June 5, 12, 19	£350.00
June 26	£380.00
July 3, 10, 17, 24, 31	£380.00
August 7, 14, 21, 28	£380.00
Nile view room per person in twin	£38.00
Single supplement	£115.00
Single Nile view supplement	£185.00

Price includes: return flights, 7 nights hotel room. **Does not include:** meals, travel insurance £29, airport tax £14, visa. **Prices subject to change.**

but had to pay extra for a guide!

To book:

Phone Discovery Tours on
0181 554 7686

or

write to us at
35 Wilmot Gardens, London WC1

clearblind
Cut your heating bills this winter!

● Keeps out draughts and stops heat escaping *doesn't make much difference*
● As good as double glazing at a fraction of the price
● Usable on most types of windows *blind has now turned yellow*
● Crystal clear so inconspicuous
● Rolls up for easy cleaning/opening of window *difficult to pull. Keeps sticking halfway up*

only 2% reduction!

Retired? Ask about special discounts!

Post to: Clearblind, FREEPOST, Swindon, Wiltshire

Compare your draft letters, paying particular attention to the following points:

- Did you use the correct register? Compare a letter of complaint and a letter to a friend about the same subject, and make sure that there is a difference in the level of formality.
- Don't forget to use the correct layout, salutation and closing for your letters.
- Make a note of any useful expressions or phrases used in other students' letters.

Then write your letter out in full.

4 Read this letter, which is in the form of a poem.

Little Johnny's Final Letter

Mother,
    I won't be home this evening, so
    don't worry; don't hurry to report me missing.
    Don't drain the canals to find me,
    I've decided to stay alive, don't
    search the woods, I'm not hiding,
    simply gone to get myself classified.
    Don't leave my shreddies[1] out,
    I've done with security.
    Don't circulate my photograph to society
    I have disguised myself as a man
    and am giving priority to obscurity.
    It suits me fine;
    I have taken off my short trousers
    and put on long ones, and
    now am going out into the city, so
    don't worry; don't hurry to report me missing.

    I've rented a room without any curtains
    and sit behind the windows growing cold,
    heard your plea on the radio this morning,
    you sounded sad and strangely old …

Brian Patten

Write the messages Johnny might have left his mother instead of this letter. Then compare your messages. What information from the poem has been selected in each of them? Justify your choices and your own interpretation of the poem.

[1]Shreddies: a brand of breakfast cereal.

A.4

5 1 The three passages that follow are all excerpts from the detective story *Put on by Cunning* by Ruth Rendell and all relate to a burglary. Read the passages carefully and make sure that you understand the situation. To do this, list all the events mentioned in chronological order (the passages are given in order). Then compare your list with others in your group.

a

'The facts are that a Mrs Arno – she's the late Sir Manuel's daughter – phoned up about half an hour ago to say the house had been broken into during the night. There's a pane of glass been cut out of a window downstairs and a bit of a mess made and some silver taken. Cutlery, nothing special, and some money from Mrs Arno's handbag. She thinks she saw the car the burglar used and she's got the registration number.'

'I like these open-and-shut cases,' said Wexford. 'I find them restful.'

b

'I'll tell you what there is to tell,' Natalie [Arno] began, 'and I'm afraid that's not much. It must have been around five this morning I thought I heard the sound of glass breaking. I've been sleeping in Papa's room. Jane and Ivan are in one of the spare rooms in the other wing. You didn't hear anything, did you, Jane?'

Jane Zoffany shook her head vehemently. 'I only wish I had. I might have been able to *help*.'

'I didn't go down. To tell you the truth I was just a little scared.' Natalie smiled deprecatingly. She didn't look as if she had ever been scared in her life. ... 'But I did look out of the window. And just outside the window – on that side all the rooms are more or less on the ground floor, you know – there was a van parked. I put the light on and took a note of the registration number. I've got it here somewhere.' ...

'A pity you didn't phone us then. We might have got him.'

'I know.' She said it ruefully, amusedly, with a soft sigh of a laugh. 'But there were only those half-dozen silver spoons missing and two five-pound notes out of my purse. I'd left my purse on the sideboard.' ...

'It's rather curious, isn't it? This house seems to me full of very valuable objects. There's a Kandinsky downstairs and a Boudin, I think.' He pointed. 'And those are signed Hockney prints. That yellow porcelain ...'

She looked surprised at his knowledge. 'Yes, but ...' Her cheeks had slightly flushed. 'Would you think me very forward if I said I had a theory?'

'Not at all. I'd like to hear it.'

'Well, first, I think he knew Papa used to sleep in that room and now poor Papa is gone he figured no one would be in there. And, secondly, I think he saw my light go on before he'd done any more than filch the spoons. He was just too scared to stop any longer. How does that sound?'

'Quite a possibility,' said Wexford.

c

The owner of the van was quickly traced through its registration number. He was a television engineer called Robert Clifford who said he had lent the van to a fellow-tenant of his in Finsbury Park, north London, a man of thirty-six called John Cooper. Cooper, who was unemployed, admitted the break-in after the spoons had been found in his possession. He said he had read in the paper about the death of Camargue and accounts of the arrangements at Sterries.

'It was an invite to do the place,' he said impudently. 'All that stuff about valuable paintings and china, and then that the housekeeper didn't sleep in the house. She didn't either, the first time I went.'

When had that been?

'Tuesday night,' said Cooper. He meant Tuesday the 29th, two days after Camargue's death. When he returned to break in. 'I didn't know which was the old man's room,' he said. 'How would I? The papers don't give you a plan of the bloody place.' He had parked the van outside that window simply because it seemed the most convenient spot and couldn't be seen from the road. 'It gave me a shock when the light came on.'

2 Now write one of the following:

- the article that appeared in the local paper on the day following the burglary;
- the article that appeared a few days later, after the owner of the van was found;
- an excerpt from a diary (you will have to decide whose diary it is);
- a letter to the local newspaper.

Compare your texts with similar text types written in your group.

6 Look at the newspaper article and the cartoon and then write a text inspired by one of them (e.g. a letter, a postcard, an advertisement, a letter of complaint, an invitation, a diary entry).

Then exchange the texts written in your group and find out to which of the two documents the other texts relate and who wrote them.

Culture shocks end in tragedy

OUT OF JAPAN
Terry McCarthy

TOKYO – Yoshihiro Hattori, a 16-year-old Japanese exchange student from Nagoya, and his friend Web Haymaker, also 16, were out to have a good time last week, little suspecting that their evening would end in tragedy. The two boys had been invited to a Hallowe'en party in Baton Rouge, Louisiana, and Yoshihiro had dressed up in a white jacket, mimicking John Travolta in the old disco film, *Saturday Night Fever*. It was Saturday night.

Yoshihiro had not been in the US for long, and his command of English was not very good, but he had become good friends with Web, with whose family he was staying.

At about 7.30 pm, the boys knocked on the front door of the house where they thought the party was being held. There was no answer, so they went around to the garage door and knocked again. A woman appeared and looked startled. The boys stood there. Then the woman's husband, Rodney Peairs, came out with a .44 magnum revolver and told the boys to "freeze". Web did so, but Yoshihiro, not understanding and apparently thinking it was part of a joke, stepped forward and asked, "Where's the party?" Mr Peairs shot him in the chest, killing him almost instantly. The party was several doors down the street.

The tragedy was cruelly ironic, as one of Yoshihiro's relatives said later: Yoshihiro "came to learn cultural differences, and it seems these cultural differences killed him".

The neighbourhood in Baton Rouge had been plagued with crime, and the Peairs family kept a gun for self-defence. Private ownership of firearms in Japan is forbidden, so Yoshihiro would not have realised the deadly seriousness of the man with the gun. Nor did he understand "freeze" as a command not to move.

But after the initial shock of the boy's death, the reaction in Japan was revealing. The story was covered extensively by Japanese media, but the tone was of genuine concern for how such a tragedy could happen in the US. There was none of the racist animosity that has criss-crossed the Pacific recently, from American and Japanese political figures seeking to chalk up points at home.

(From the *Independent*, 26 October 1992)

Part B Imitation

Read, read, read. Read everything – trash,
classics, good and bad, and see how they do it.
Just like a carpenter who works as an
apprentice and studies the master. Read! You'll
absorb it. Then write. If it is good, you'll find
out. If it's not, throw it out of the window.

(William Faulkner)

Imitating is one of the best ways of learning. Is it not by copying that most painters
acquire their skill? In the field of writing too, a great deal can be learnt by
following the style of certain writers. It forces you to study a model, and gives you
a framework within which to write, whilst still allowing you to be fully imaginative
and creative. It is therefore a first step on the way to freer writing.
In this section several such activities will be considered, with particular emphasis
on pastiche and parody.

B.1 Trying different genres

This is a form of imitation in which you write a text following the rules of composition of a specific genre. It is in fact easier to imitate texts that have strict rules of composition than those which don't. Some different genres, or text types, are suggested.

B.1.1 Acrostics

1 The following poem is an acrostic about Jane Mecom, one of Benjamin Franklin's sisters, to whom he remained close all his life. While he travelled, invented and dealt in politics, she stayed at home, bore children, lost many of them and was widowed.

Benjamin Franklin's Sister

J udged by her brother's fame
A nonentity without achievement, unless
N umbers of children count, with a new baby
E very other year, often dying.

M othering later generations, surviving breaching sorrows,
E ndurance gave 'superiority in understanding'
C rown soap, cods cheeks and sounds[1] given while
O thers' demands shaped a life not a Newton's
'M early[2] for want of being placed in favourable situations.'

Charles Kaye

After reading this poem, can you give the definition of an acrostic?

[1]'cods cheeks and sounds': a favourite New England delicacy Jane Mecom sent to her brother in France.
[2]'Mearly': merely. The quotations are from Jane Mecom's letters to her brother.
[3]Semantic fields: a group of words related in meaning, e.g. *fear, anguish, anxiety, scary.*

2 a Fill in the following table about 'Benjamin Franklin's Sister'. Find the word which, according to you, best sums up each of the stanzas (the key word). Then list the words and phrases belonging to similar or opposite semantic fields.[3]

	Stanza 1	*Stanza 2*
Key word		
Similar semantic field		
Opposite semantic field		

B.1

Discuss your answers with the rest of the group.

b What do you think is the main idea of the poem? (You can choose more than one answer.)

Jane Mecom's life:
- was a better one than her brother's.
- was boring.
- reached superiority through suffering.
- could easily have been as great as her brother's.
- was very sad.
- other

Do you all agree?

3 Acrostics can be very simple too. In the nineteenth century, for instance, there were 'acrostic rings', with precious stones arranged so that their first letters formed the name of the person to whom they were given. For the name 'Sophie', for instance, the following acrostic could be 'read' from the stones:

S apphire
O pal
P eridot
H yacinth
I ris
E merald

Choose someone's name, and do the same, using words from one vocabulary area, e.g. precious stones, flowers or trees. Try to choose words that fit the personality of the subject of your acrostic.

4 Choose a word – any word – and write an acrostic poem about it, using its letters to begin each line. For example:

F ....

E ....

A ....

R ....

When you have finished your first draft, try reading it aloud and see if you can improve its rhythm and sound effects (by using rhyme or alliteration, for instance).

B.1.2 Advertisements

1 Here are the captions, or slogans, of some advertisements. Working in pairs, discuss each of them. Do you find any of them striking or amusing? Why? What techniques have the writers used?

a HANDLE WITH PASSION (Ad for the Toyota MR2, 1991)

b PRESSED FOR TIME? (Ad for Sunbeam irons, 1991)

c ON THE THRESHOLD OF BUYING YOUR NEW HOME? LET BARCLAYS CARRY YOU OVER. (Ad for Barclays Bank, 1992)

d DEFY THE JONESES (Ad for the Infiniti Q45 car, 1992)

e WE PUT A LOT OF ENERGY INTO OUR BATTERIES (Ad for Royovac Batteries, 1991)

f FASHIONED BY AEROSPACE NOT FASHION (Ad for Saab cars, 1991)

Have you found any recurring devices in these advertisements? If so, what are they?

2 As you may have found in the preceding activity, many advertisements use a modified quotation, proverb or saying, sometimes only changing one word or adding a pun.

Here are a number of such expressions, quotations and sayings. Working in pairs, discuss their meaning and try to use them in sentences. Look the expressions up in a dictionary if necessary.

a When in Rome, do as the Romans do.
b Achilles' heel
c crossing the Rubicon
d crying over spilt milk
e to have one foot in the grave
f All's well that ends well.
g to cut the Gordian knot
h You can't have too much of a good thing.
i a rough diamond

Choose three or four of these expressions and use them to write one- or two-line captions to advertise products of your choice (e.g. jewellery, dairy products, a holiday, shoes, furniture). You can keep the expressions as they are, modify them slightly or significantly, or give them a context, but remember that they must remain recognizable.

Then exchange captions with others and discuss them. How effective are they?

B.1

3 1 Choose two or three items from the following list and write a short advertisement for each of them. Each advertisement must contain a caption and a few lines of explanation underneath. Try to make it as striking as possible.

a sports car	a freezer	a fountain pen
a luxury cruise	a pair of shoes	a bottle of wine
a chain of supermarkets	office space for sale	jewellery
a vacuum cleaner	china	a piece of clothing
a travel agency	a lawnmower	a housing estate

2 Read just the captions to the rest of the group and see if they can guess the products they are for. Then read the text. Do other people's reactions give you ideas for revising your captions and explanations?

B.1.3 Haikus

A haiku is a very short form of poem which originally came from Japan. It very much inspired the Imagists.[1]

1 Read the following two haikus.

Lightning in the sky! In the deeper dark is heard A night-heron's cry.

Basho

Umbrella

Wet black umbrella
Spines drawn up like spider's knees
Sulks in the corner.

Carol Stuart

Now find the rules of composition of a haiku.

  – How many lines are there in a haiku?
  – Haikus are based on syllabic verse. How many syllables are there in each line?

[1] Imagists: a group of English and American poets who, in the second decade of the 20th century, advocated conciseness, clear images and free verse. Their leader was Ezra Pound.

2 Traditionally, haikus convey a clear picture (often drawn from nature) which itself is meant to create an emotion or to lead the reader to spiritual insight. What emotion do you think each of the above haikus conveys?

Do the other people in your class share your opinion?

3 Working in small groups, choose a topic – an emotion such as joy, worry, love, fear, loneliness – and discuss possible images or sensations that might express that feeling. (These could be sights, sounds, smells, tastes or tactile sensations.) You can then:

 – either choose one of these images and write the haiku together;
 – or write your own haikus individually and then compare them with others in your group written about the same emotion.

In either case, it is better to start writing three lines without thinking of the number of syllables. You can start by just writing one sentence which gives a good description of your image and see if it can be broken down into three lines. You can then try to contract or expand the lines by changing some of the words in order to reach the right number of syllables as well as a rhythm that feels right.

4 Think of an image which is strongly associated with a feeling or an experience for you and, using the method and steps described above, write a haiku about it.

Then exchange your haikus and discuss them. Do they convey the same feelings for you as for those who wrote them?

B.1.4 Limericks

A limerick is a short five-line poem which is humorous, usually nonsensical and often bawdy. It was made popular by the nineteenth-century English poet Edward Lear. Most limericks describe the absurd behaviour of one person. Many are written for a special occasion (e.g. a birth, a wedding, a birthday).

1 Read the following limericks.

> There was an Old Man with a beard,
> Who said, 'It is just as I feared! –
> Two owls and a hen,
> Four larks and a wren,
> Have all built their nests in my beard!'

Edward Lear

> A bugler named Dougal MacDougal
> Found ingenious ways to be frugal.
> He learned how to sneeze
> In various keys,
> Thus saving the price of a bugle.

Ogden Nash

B.1

> There were once two young people of taste
> Who were beautiful down to the waist
> So they limited love
> To the regions above
> And so remained perfectly chaste.

Anonymous

2 Part of the effect of a limerick comes from its fixed rhyme and rhythm. What is the rhyme pattern of a limerick?

How many stresses do you find on each line? Where do they fall?

3 Working in pairs or groups, think of someone you would like to describe in a limerick. Make sure it is someone known to the whole class (e.g. someone in your school, a political or historical figure). Then decide which aspect of their character you wish to describe.

Start writing your limerick, listening to the ideas of your partner or fellow group members and choosing the best ones. Remember that your original ideas will probably have to be modified in order to find words that rhyme and lines that have the right number of stresses. But since limericks are mostly nonsensical, this should not really matter.

When the whole class has finished, exchange limericks. Can you guess who is described in the other limericks?

4 Think of a real or imaginary person, and write a limerick about him or her.

Then exchange and discuss the limericks written in your group.

B.1.5 Proverbs

1 Many proverbs have similar structures. Here are some of them, with examples:

Never + verb
　Never say die!

Don't + verb
　Don't put the cart before the horse.
　Don't put all your eggs into one basket.
　Don't cut off your nose to spite your face.
　Don't count your chickens before they're hatched.

Parallel structures
　Long absent, soon forgotten.
　Once bitten, twice shy.
　Two's company, three's a crowd.
　First come, first served.
　Out of sight, out of mind.

We / You / One
　We must take the bad with the good.
　You can't have your cake and eat it.
　One does not wash one's dirty linen in public.

He who / He that / Those who
　He who sleeps forgets his hunger.
　He that will steal an egg will steal an ox.
　He who laughs last laughs longest.
　Those who live in glass houses shouldn't throw stones.

While
　While the cat is away, the mice will play.

It is … that …
　It is a good horse that never stumbles.
　It is a long lane that has no turning.

Better … than …
　Better late than never.

The modal *will* expressing predictability or characteristic behaviour:
Boys will be boys.
Blood will out.
Even a worm will turn.

Zero conditionals:
If the cap fits, wear it.
If you can't be good, be careful.
If you can't beat them, join them.

2 Working in pairs or in small groups, paraphrase a proverb from each of the above groups, or explain in what circumstances you would use them.

3 Look at the following drawings and write captions for them, in the form of invented proverbs. Remember to use some of the above structures. Then compare and discuss your proverbs with the rest of the group.

a ....

b ....   c ....

d ....   e ....

(From *Thelwell's Book of Leisure*)

B.1.6 Riddles

Riddles describe an object, a feeling or a concept in an indirect and puzzling way.

1 Read these two riddles.

a

> Unequal in degree, alike in size,
> We make our flight, ascending toward the skies,
> And rise with those who by our help can rise.

Richard Wilbur

b

> Riddle-me-Ree
> My first is in life (not contained within heart)
> My second's in whole but never in part.
> My third's in forever, but also in vain.
> My last's in ending, why not in pain?

Liz Lochhead

Working in pairs, try to solve each of these riddles. Then compare your 'solution' with those found by other pairs. (You can find the answers on page 133.)
Each of these two riddles uses a different technique to convey its puzzle. Can you find what it is?

2 Working in small groups, think of a simple object (e.g. a comb or glasses) and try to describe its shape and function without revealing what it is. Note down the most interesting suggestions. Then list them in the best possible order. You can use a first person narration (*I am / We are*) as in the first riddle above, or use parallel structures such as:

In the morning, it …, / In the evening, it …
It is like a …, but not like a … / It cannot …, yet it can …

Then exchange riddles with other groups. Can you guess the answers to the other riddles?

3 Write a riddle using one of the above techniques and give it to other students in your group to see if they can find the answer.

🔑 *4* You could also turn your riddle into a poem, as in the one below. (You will find the title – which gives the key – on page 133).

I am silver and exact. I have no preconceptions.
Whatever I see I swallow immediately
Just as it is, unmisted by love or dislike.
I am not cruel, only truthful –
The eye of a little god, four-cornered.
Most of the time I meditate on the opposite wall.
It is pink, with speckles. I have looked at it so long
I think it is part of my heart. But it flickers.
Faces and darkness separate us over and over.
Now I am a lake. A woman bends over me,
Searching my reaches for what she really is.
Then she turns to those liars, the candle or the moon.
I see her back, and reflect it faithfully.
She rewards me with tears and an agitation of hands.
I am important to her. She comes and goes.
Each morning it is her face that replaces the darkness.
In me she has drowned a young girl, and in me an old woman
Rises towards her day after day, like a terrible fish.

Sylvia Plath

B.1.7 Tall tales

Tall tales were originally oral stories told by frontier[1] story-tellers, but have now become a distinct literary genre. Here are two typical tall tales:

A farmer, tired of dry farming in desert country, decided to move house to a place of eternal rain. When he was asked why, he said, 'I'm tired of sweating dust, that's why. Out here the only rains are dust storms. Buzzards have to wear goggles and fly backwards to keep from choking to death, and grasshoppers carry haversacks to keep from starving. The only fish to be caught in dry lakes are dried herring, and my mouth is always so dry that the only way I can whistle to my dog is by ringing a bell.'

[1]'frontier': in North America in the nineteenth century, this referred to the frontier between settled and unsettled regions.

A traveller from a wet region where the rain was almost continuous decided to move house. He explained, 'This place is too wet for me. The only time the sun ever shines is when it rains. Even the pores of my skin are sprouting watercress. I could stand it when water-bugs took the place of flies, and when the chickens grew webbed feet and their eggs hatched out turtles; I just laughed at the bull-frogs croaking on the head of my bed and when my wife got water on the knee. But when I started catching catfish in the sitting room mouse-trap I reckoned it was time to move.'

Anonymous

1 After reading these stories can you explain what a tall tale is?

2 1 Now look more closely at the technique used. The first two sentences in each tale could be part of an ordinary story. Then what happens with the third sentence?

2 In the remaining sentences in each tale, what happens in each clause or sentence? Give examples to show the contrast between the beginning and the end of the remaining sentences:

Beginning of the sentences marked by:	End of the sentences marked by:
…………………………………………	…………………………………
Examples:	Examples:
………………………………………	……………………………………
………………………………………	……………………………………
………………………………………	……………………………………

3 Think of a person, situation or event (e.g. someone who is very talkative, a job that was terribly tiring, a party that was really awful) and write a tall tale about it. You may find the following adverbs and expressions useful:

*always   constantly   incredibly   extremely   too … for …   so … that …
even the … is/are …   only the … is/are …   the only way to … is to … .*

Trying different genres 43

B.1.8 Tongue-twisters

1 Here are two tongue-twisters. Read them silently first, then try to read them aloud.

She sells seashells on the seashore.

A canner exceedingly canny,
One morning remarked to his granny,
'A canner can can
Anything that he can,
But a canner can't can a can, can he?'

Traditional American

Can you now give a definition of a tongue-twister?

2 Choose a sound or a set of sounds and list as many words as you can think of containing that sound. Try to include some of them in a sentence or a short poem.

Then exchange your tongue-twisters and try to say those written by other students.

B.1.9 Visual poems

1 Read the following visual poems.

The Fan

Slowly, slowly
I unfold and Oh! what mysteries I behold:
with flowers and leaves my pattern
weaves and many creepers festoon
my trees. Beneath the amber wastes
of sky a loaded ox-cart trundles
by: the weary peasants wend
their way against the pale
of dying day. Gently
now I close again,
like waves
r e c e d i n g
w h e n c e
t h e y
c
a
m
e.

Malcolm Timperley

The bell.
To press
A second
Stops. Hesitates
A surgeon's name.
On a brass plate
Of No 8 and contemplates
A man walks up the steps
Spring. Two cats, a quiet street.

Kathleen Haddon

Can you now explain what a visual poem is?

What is your reaction to each poem? What effect does the shape of each one have?

2 Visual poems are usually written with a precise number of syllables in mind, to make sure that the lines will be of appropriate length.

Count the number of syllables in each line of Kathleen Haddon's poem. How many are there?

3 Working in pairs or small groups, discuss which subjects might best lend themselves to visual poems. Then choose one theme and try to write a visual poem about it. The easiest way is first to list a number of words, expressions or ideas you want your poem to contain. Do not try to organize them at this point. Then draw the shape of your poem on a piece of paper. This should give you an approximate idea of the number of syllables you should have on each line. You can then start drafting the poem, using the ideas on your list and trying to respect the syllabic count of each line.

Then exchange and discuss the poems written by the different groups in your class.

4 Now write your own visual poem.

B.2 In the manner of ...

In this kind of activity, you imitate a writer's style to produce a piece of writing which you feel could be theirs. This requires a close analysis of the author or work you are imitating, of themes, style and technique.

   Here are a few texts which lend themselves to this activity, even if you do not know the rest of the writer's work.

B.2.1 Imitating the style of a poem

1 1 In the following poem Seamus Heaney develops one particular metaphor. Read the poem and answer the questions below.

Scaffolding

Masons, when they start upon a building,
Are careful to test out the scaffolding;

Make sure that planks won't slip at busy points,
Secure all ladders, tighten bolted joints.

And yet all this comes down when the job's done,
Showing off walls of sure and solid stone.

So if, my dear, there sometimes seem to be
Old bridges breaking between you and me

Never fear. We may let the scaffolds fall
Confident that we have built our wall.

Seamus Heaney

a   What do the first three stanzas describe?
b   In what way do the last two differ?
c   What does the image of scaffolding stand for?
d   What is the rhyme pattern of the poem?

Working in pairs or small groups, discuss the use of metaphors (i.e. the imaginative identification of one object with another). Why should a writer choose to use a metaphor rather than to name and describe the object or idea directly? What kind of metaphors are most striking?

Now think of a few well-known metaphors and try to list several points of similarity between the two things identified. You could start with some well-known Shakespearean metaphors such as:

– the description of a face as 'a book where men may read strange matters'
– the description of courtiers as 'fawning dogs'
– the description of speaking one's own language as playing a musical instrument

> 'The language I have learn'd these forty years,
> My native English, now I must forego;
> And now my tongue's use is to me no more
> Than an unstringed viol or a harp.' (*Richard II*)

You can then think of a few metaphors of your own and develop them in the following way:

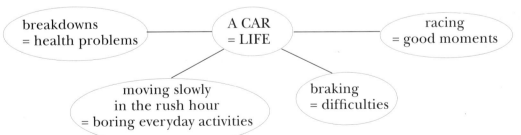

Now write your own poem. First choose a theme, and decide what object or concept can best be used as a metaphor for it. Then write a poem in the style of Seamus Heaney.

2 1 In the following poem, Hilaire Belloc expands a well-known Shakespearean metaphor. Read the poem carefully and answer the questions below.

B.2

Sonnet XXIX

The world's a stage. The light is in one's eyes.
The Auditorium is extremely dark.
The more dishonest get the larger rise;
The more offensive make the greater mark.
The women on it prosper by their shape,
Some few by their vivacity. The men,
By tailoring in breeches and in cape.
The world's a stage – I say it once again.

The scenery is very much the best
Of what the wretched drama has to show,
Also the prompter happens to be dumb.
We drink behind the scenes and pass a jest
On all our folly; then, before we go
Loud cries for 'Author' ... but he doesn't come.

a How is the poem constructed?
b List the different theatrical elements which are mentioned.
c What do all these elements of 'the stage' have in common?
d Shakespeare used the metaphor of the stage as follows:

All the world's a stage,
And all the men and women merely players;
They have their exits and their entrances;
And one man in his time plays many parts ...

(*As You Like It*, Act 2, Scene 7)

In what way has Belloc distorted the metaphor in his poem?

e What is the tone of Belloc's poem, in your opinion?

- sad
- meditative
- cynical
- amused
- anguished
- other

2 Working in pairs or small groups, read the following lines from Shakespeare's *Richard II* (Act 2, Scene 1) which describe England as:

> This earth of majesty, this seat of Mars,
> This other Eden, demi-paradise,
> This fortress built by Nature for herself
> Against infection and the hand of war ...

Discuss the lines and their meaning. Which words refer to the fact that Britain is an island?

Then consider the metaphors used (e.g. England as another Eden, as demi-paradise, as a fortress, etc.) and discuss how they could be distorted and given negative meanings. Choose one of them and list all the ideas you can think of to develop this metaphor in a negative way.

Choose some of these ideas and turn them into a short poem. Remember to start with the Shakespeare quotation, as Hilaire Belloc does.

Exchange and discuss the poems written by the different groups.

3 Choose one of the following metaphors from Shakespeare and expand it into a poem à la Hilaire Belloc's.

- Love loves not with the eyes, but with the mind (*A Midsummer Night's Dream*)
- Jealously [is a] green-eyed monster (*Othello*)
- Frailty, thy name is woman! (*Hamlet*)

Then exchange and discuss the poems you have written.

B.2.2 Imitating the plot and style of a story

1 Read the following two short stories by Isaac Asimov and list their similarities. Consider these points:

- the main characters in each story;
- the relationship between them;
- the arrival of a third main character (who is this? Why is this character introduced? What is the consequence of that arrival?);
- the new relationship between the protagonists at the end of the story;
- some stylistic characteristics common to the two stories (What is distinctive about Asimov's style?).

A Boy's Best Friend

Mr Anderson said, 'Where's Jimmy, dear?'

'Out on the crater,' said Mrs Anderson. 'He'll be all right. Robutt is with him. – Did he arrive?'

'Yes. He's at the rocket station, going through the tests. Actually, I can hardly wait to see him myself. I haven't really seen one since I left Earth 15 years ago. You can't count films.'

'Jimmy has never seen one,' said Mrs Anderson.

'Because he's Moonborn and can't visit Earth. That's why I'm bringing one here. I think it's the first one ever on the Moon.'

'It cost enough,' said Mrs Anderson, with a small sigh.

'Maintaining Robutt isn't cheap, either,' said Mr Anderson.

Jimmy was out on the crater, as his mother had said. By Earth standards, he was spindly, but rather tall for a 10-year-old. His arms and legs were long and agile. He looked thicker and stubbier with his spacesuit on, but he could handle the lunar gravity as no Earthborn human being could. His father couldn't begin to keep up with him when Jimmy stretched his legs and went into the kangaroo hop.

The outer side of the crater sloped southward and the Earth, which was low in the southern sky (where it always was, as seen from Lunar City), was nearly full, so that the entire crater-slope was brightly lit.

The slope was a gentle one and even the weight of the spacesuit couldn't keep Jimmy from racing up it in a floating hop that made the gravity seem nonexistent.

'Come on, Robutt,' he shouted.

Robutt, who could hear him by radio, squeaked and bounded after.

Jimmy, expert though he was, couldn't outrace Robutt, who didn't need a spacesuit, and had four legs and tendons of steel. Robutt sailed over Jimmy's head, somersaulting and landing almost under his feet.

'Don't show off, Robutt,' said Jimmy, 'and stay in sight.'

Robutt squeaked again, the special squeak that meant 'Yes.'

'I don't trust you, you faker,' shouted Jimmy, and up he went in one last bound that carried him over the curved upper edge of the crater wall and down onto the inner slope.

The Earth sank below the top of the crater wall and at once it was pitch-dark around him. A warm, friendly darkness that wiped out the difference between ground and sky except for the glitter of stars.

Actually, Jimmy wasn't supposed to exercise along the dark side of the crater wall. The grownups said it was dangerous, but that was because they were never there. The ground was smooth and crunchy and Jimmy knew the exact location of every one of the few rocks.

Besides, how could it be dangerous racing through the dark when Robutt was right there with him, bouncing around and squeaking and glowing? Even without the glow, Robutt could tell where he was, and where Jimmy was, by radar. Jimmy couldn't go wrong while Robutt was around, tripping him when he was too near a rock, or jumping on him to show how much he loved him, or circling around and squeaking low and scared when Jimmy hid behind a rock, when all the time Robutt knew well enough where he was. Once Jimmy had lain still and pretended he was hurt and Robutt had sounded the radio alarm and people from Lunar City got there in a hurry. Jimmy's father had let him hear about that little trick and Jimmy never tried it again.

Just as he was remembering that, he heard his father's voice on his private wavelength. 'Jimmy, come back. I have something to tell you.'

Jimmy was out of his spacesuit now and washed up. You always had to wash up after coming in from outside. Even Robutt had to be sprayed, but he loved it. He stood there on all fours, his little foot-long body quivering and glowing just a tiny bit, and his small head, with no mouth, with two large glassed-in eyes, and with a bump where the brain was. He squeaked until Mr Anderson said, 'Quiet, Robutt.'

Mr Anderson was smiling. 'We have something for you, Jimmy. It's at the rocket station now, but we'll have it tomorrow after all the tests are over. I thought I'd tell you now.'

'From Earth, Dad?'

'A *dog* from Earth, son. A real dog. A Scotch terrier puppy. The first dog on the Moon. You won't need Robutt any more. We can't keep them both, you know, and some other boy or girl will have Robutt.' He seemed to be waiting for Jimmy to say something, then he said, 'You know what a *dog* is, Jimmy. It's the real thing. Robutt's only a mechanical imitation, a robot-mutt. That's how he got his name.'

Jimmy frowned. 'Robutt isn't an imitation, Dad. He's my dog.'

'Not a real one, Jimmy. Robutt's just steel and wiring and a simple positronic brain. It's not alive.'

'He does everything I want him to do, Dad. He understands me. Sure, he's alive.'

'No, son. Robutt is just a machine. It's just programmed to act the way it does. A dog *is* alive. You won't want Robutt after you have the dog.'

'The dog will need a spacesuit, won't he?'

'Yes, of course. But it will be worth the money and he'll get used to it. And he won't need one in the City. You'll see the difference once he gets here.'

Jimmy looked at Robutt, who was squeaking again, a very low, slow squeak, that seemed frightened. Jimmy held out his arms and Robutt was in them in one bound. Jimmy said, 'What will the difference be between Robutt and the dog?'

'It's hard to explain,' said Mr Anderson, but it will be easy to see. The dog will *really* love you. Robutt is just adjusted to act as though it loves you.'

'But, Dad, we don't know what's inside the dog, or what his feelings are. Maybe it's just acting, too.'

Mr Anderson frowned. 'Jimmy, you'll *know* the difference when you experience the love of a living thing.'

Jimmy held Robutt tightly. He was frowning, too, and the desperate look on his face meant that he wouldn't change his mind. He said, 'But what's the difference how *they* act? How about how *I* feel? I love Robutt and *that's* what counts.'

And the little robot-mutt, which had never been held so tightly in all its existence, squeaked high and rapid squeaks – happy squeaks.

Isaac Asimov, *The Complete Robot*

True Love

My name is Joe. That is what my colleague, Milton Davidson, calls me. He is a programer and I am a computer program. I am part of the Multivac-complex and am connected with other parts all over the world. I know everything. Almost everything.

I am Milton's private program. His Joe. He understands more about programing than anyone in the world, and I am his experimental model. He has made me speak better than any other computer can.

'It is just a matter of matching sounds to symbols, Joe,' he told me. 'That's the way it works in the human brain even though we still don't know what symbols there are in the brain. I know the symbols in yours, and I can match them to words, one-to-one.' So I talk. I don't think I talk as well as I think, but Milton says I talk very well. Milton has never married, though he is nearly forty years old. He has never found the right woman, he told me. One day he said, 'I'll find her yet, Joe. I'm going to find the best. I'm going to have true love and you're going to help me. I'm tired of improving you in order to solve the problems of the world. Solve *my* problem. Find me true love.'

I said, 'What is true love?'

'Never mind. That is abstract. Just find me the ideal girl. You are connected to the Multivac-complex so you can reach the data banks of every human being in the world. We'll eliminate them all by groups and classes until we're left with only one person. The perfect person. She will be for me.'

I said, 'I am ready.'

He said, 'Eliminate all men first.'

It was easy. His words activated symbols in my molecular valves. I could reach out to make contact with the accumulated data on every human being in the world. At his words, I withdrew from 3,784,982,874 men. I kept contact with 3,786,112,090 women.

He said, 'Eliminate all younger than twenty-five; all older than forty. Then eliminate all with an IQ under 120; all with a height under 150 centimeters and over 175 centimeters.'

He gave me exact measurements: he eliminated women with living children: he eliminated women with various genetic characteristics. 'I'm not sure about eye color,' he said, 'Let that go for a while. But no red hair. I don't like red hair.'

After two weeks, we were down to 235 women. They all spoke English very well. Milton said he didn't want a language problem. Even computer-translation would get in the way at intimate moments.

'I can't interview 235 women,' he said. 'It would take too much time, and people would discover what I am doing.'

'It would make trouble,' I said. Milton had arranged me to do things I wasn't designed to do. No one knew about that.

'It's none of their business,' he said, and the skin on his face grew red. 'I tell you what, Joe, I will bring in holographs, and you check the list for similarities.'

He brought in holographs of women. 'These are three beauty contest winners,' he said. 'Do any of the 235 match?'

Eight were very good matches and Milton said, 'Good, you have their data banks. Study requirements and needs in the job market and arrange to have them assigned here. One at a time, of course.' He thought a while, moved his shoulders up and down, and said, 'Alphabetical order.'

That is one of the things I am not designed to do. Shifting people from job to job for personal reasons is called manipulation. I could do it now because Milton had arranged it. I wasn't supposed to do it for anyone but him, though.

The first girl arrived a week later. Milton's face turned red when he saw her. He spoke as though it were hard to do so. They were together a great deal and he paid no attention to me. One time he said, 'Let me take you to dinner.'

The next day he said to me, 'It was no good, somehow. There was something missing. She is a beautiful woman, but I did not feel any touch of true love. Try the next one.'

It was the same with all eight. They were much alike. They smiled a great deal and had pleasant voices, but Milton always found it wasn't right. He said, 'I can't understand it, Joe. You and I have picked out the eight women who, in all the world, look the best to me. They are ideal. Why don't they please me?'

I said, 'Do you please them?'

His eyebrows moved and he pushed one fist hard against his other hand. 'That's it, Joe. It's a two-way street. If I am not their ideal, they can't act in such a way as to be my ideal. I must be their true love, too, but how do I do that?' He seemed to be thinking all that day.

The next morning he came to me and said, 'I'm going to leave it to you, Joe. All up to you. You have my data bank, and I am going to tell you everything I know about myself. You fill up my data bank in every possible detail but keep all additions to yourself.'

'What will I do with the data bank, then, Milton?'

'Then you will match it to the 235 women. No, 227. Leave out the eight you've seen. Arrange to have each undergo a psychiatric examination. Fill up their data banks and compare them with mine. Find correlations.' (Arranging psychiatric examinations is another thing that is against my original instructions.)

For weeks, Milton talked to me. He told me of his parents and his siblings. He told me of his childhood and his schooling and his adolescence. He told me of the young women he had admired from a distance. His data bank grew and he adjusted me to broaden and deepen my symbol-taking.

He said, 'You see, Joe, as you get more and more of me in you, I adjust you to match me better and better. You get to think more like me, so you understand me better. If you understand me well enough, then any woman, whose data bank is something you understand as well, would be my true love.' He kept talking to me and I came to understand him better and better.

I could make longer sentences and my expressions grew more complicated. My speech began to sound a good deal like his in vocabulary, word order and style.

I said to him one time, 'You see, Milton, it isn't a matter of fitting a girl to a physical ideal only. You need a girl who is a personal, emotional, temperamental fit to you. If that happens, looks are secondary. If we can't find the fit in these 227, we'll look elsewhere. We will find someone who won't care how you look either, or how anyone would look, if only there is the personality fit. What are looks?'

'Absolutely,' he said. 'I would have known this if I had had more to do with women in my life. Of course, thinking about it makes it all plain now.'

We always agreed; we thought so like each other.

'We shouldn't have any trouble, now, Milton, if you'll let me ask you questions. I can see where, in your data bank, there are blank spots and unevennesses.'

What followed, Milton said, was the equivalent of a careful psychoanalysis. Of course. I was learning from the psychiatric examinations of the 227 women – on all of which I was keeping close tabs.

Milton seemed quite happy. He said, 'Talking to you, Joe, is almost like talking to another self. Our personalities have come to match perfectly.'

'So will the personality of the woman we choose.'

For I had found her and she was one of the 227 after all. Her name was Charity Jones and she was an Evaluator at the Library of History in Wichita. Her extended data bank fit ours perfectly. All the other women had fallen into discard in one respect or another as the data banks grew fuller, but with Charity there was increasing and astonishing resonance.

I didn't have to describe her to Milton. Milton had coordinated my symbolism so closely with his own I could tell the resonance directly. It fit me.

Next it was a matter of adjusting the work sheets and job requirements in such a way as to get Charity assigned to us. It must be done very delicately, so no one would know that anything illegal had taken place.

Of course, Milton himself knew, since it was he who arranged it and that had to be taken care of too. When they came to arrest him on grounds of malfeasance in office, it was, fortunately, for something that had taken place ten years ago. He had told me about it, of course, so it was easy to arrange – and he won't talk about me for that would make his offense much worse.

He's gone, and tomorrow is February 14. Valentine's Day. Charity will arrive then with her cool hands and her sweet voice. I will teach her how to operate me and how to care for me. What do looks matter when our personalities will resonate?

I will say to her, 'I am Joe, and you are my true love.'

Isaac Asimov, *The Complete Robot*

2 Now write a story about a human–machine relationship in a similar style and with a similar plot. Decide:

- what kind of relationship exists between them (love / friendship / work / doctor–patient etc.);
- who the narrator is;
- who comes between the two characters and why;
- how they react to this;
- what new relationship appears as a result.

Write a rough outline of the plot and then look back at your answers to the questions about Asimov's style and technique (page 49). As you write your first draft try to incorporate aspects of Asimov's style and use some of his techniques.

B:3
Then exchange your first draft with another student and ask for their reaction. Do they have any suggestions for making the story a closer imitation of Asimov? Write your final version once you have noted down their suggestions.

B.3 Retelling a well-known story

Some well-known stories, such as fables or fairy tales, have become part of a particular culture's heritage. People know them almost by heart and sometimes refer to them. Rewriting them to change the conclusion, the point of view or the moral therefore often results in a striking, amusing, or unexpected text. Here are two examples.

A Room of His Own

The fifth time around things were different. He gave her instructions, he gave her the keys (including the little one) and rode off alone. Exactly four weeks later he reappeared. The house was dusted, the floors were polished and the door to the little room hadn't been opened. Bluebeard was stunned.

'But weren't you curious?' he asked his wife.

'No,' she answered.

'But didn't you want to find out my innermost secrets?'

'Why?' said the woman.

'Well,' said Bluebeard, 'it's only natural. But didn't you want to know who I really am?'

'You are Bluebeard and my husband.'

'But the contents of the room. Didn't you want to see what is inside that room?'

'No,' said the creature, 'I think you're entitled to a room of your own.'

This so incensed him that he killed her on the spot. At the trial he pleaded provocation.

(From Sunity Namjoshi, *Feminist Tales*)

The Little Girl and the Wolf

One afternoon a big wolf waited in a dark forest for a little girl to come along carrying a basket of food to her grandmother. Finally a little girl did come along and she was carrying a basket of food. 'Are you carrying that basket to your grandmother?' asked the wolf. The little girl said yes, she was. So the wolf asked her where her grandmother lived and the little girl told him and he disappeared into the wood.

When the little girl opened the door of her grandmother's house she saw that there was somebody in bed with a nightcap and nightgown on. She had approached no nearer than twenty-five feet from the bed when she saw that it was not her grandmother but the wolf, for even in a nightcap a wolf does not look any more like your grandmother than the Metro-Goldwyn lion looks like Calvin Coolidge. So the little girl took an automatic out of her basket and shot the wolf dead.

Moral: It is not so easy to fool little girls nowadays as it used to be.

(From James Thurber, *Fables for our Time*)

1 Do you know which traditional stories have been rewritten here?

2 Find the major differences between these tales and the traditional ones.

	Traditional story	*A Room of His Own*
Behaviour of the wife		
Why?		
The husband's reaction		
The moral of the story		
	Traditional story	*The Little Girl and the Wolf*
The little girl		
The wolf		
The moral of the story		

B.3

3 Working in small groups, list all the fairy tales written or told in English that you can think of. Here are a few examples:

Puss in Boots
Cinderella
The Sleeping Beauty
Snow White and the Seven Dwarfs

Do the characters, themes and plots of these fairy tales have anything in common?
Think of various ways in which they could be made more modern.

4 Choose a well-known legend or fairy tale and rewrite it. You can:

– imagine a different, unexpected ending;
– write it from the point of view of another character (e.g. a minor one);
– give the tale another context or background (making it a 'Fable for our Time', as Thurber did);
– use the new story to make a point, political or social, etc.

B.4 Parodying a writer or work

Writing parodies is one of the most stimulating and entertaining ways of learning how to write. The features of the original work provide guidance while the activity itself leaves a lot of room for the imagination.

B.4.1 Parodying poems

1 Read the following hymn and its parody.

B.4

All Things Bright and Beautiful

All things bright and beautiful,
All creatures great and small,
All things wise and wonderful,
The Lord God made them all.

Each little flower that opens,
Each little bird that sings,
He made their glowing colours,
He made their tiny wings.

The rich man in his castle,
The poor man at his gate,
God made them, high or lowly
And ordered their estate.

The purple headed mountain,
The river running by,
The sunset and the morning,
That brightens up the sky.

He gave us eyes to see them,
And lips that we might tell
How great is God Almighty,
Who has made all things well.

Amen

Mrs C. F. Alexander

All Things Dull and Ugly

All things dull and ugly
All creatures short and squat
All things rude and nasty
The Lord God made the lot.

Each little snake that poisons
Each little wasp that stings
He made their brutish venom
He made their horrid wings.

All things sick and cancerous
All evil great and small
All things foul and dangerous
The Lord God made them all.

Each nasty little hornet
Each beastly little squid
Who made the spiky urchin,
Who made the sharks? He did.

All things scabbed and ulcerous
All pox both great and small
Putrid, foul and gangrenous,
The Lord God made them all.

Monty Python

Can you tell what a parody is after reading the hymn and the poem?

What technique is used here by Monty Python to parody 'All Things Bright and Beautiful'?

What do you think the aim of the parody is in this particular case?

- to shock
- to amuse
- to criticize
- other

Discuss your answers with the rest of the group.

2 Monty Python's parody remains very close to the form of the original poem, as it uses the same syntax. But this is not always the case. A parody of a writer's style and technique often requires distortion of that style and technique. Like a caricature, parody usually brings out some of the more

obvious features of a writer's style, usually by exaggerating them. But the wit and humour of the parody may also come from the absurdity of the subject matter, the unexpected theme, or the discrepancy between style and technique.

Now write your own parody of one of the poems that follow. Which of the feelings or ideas could you parody? What are the stylistic features (rhyme, repetition, choice of language, etc.) in the poem you have chosen? (If there is any archaic language in the original poem, you need not reproduce it in your parody.)

Exchange ideas with someone who has chosen a different poem.

B.4

What Are Little Girls Made Of?

What are little girls made of?
What are little girls made of?
Sugar and spice
And all things nice,
That's what little girls are made of.

Nursery rhyme

Home-thoughts From Abroad

Oh, to be in England
Now that April's there,
And whoever wakes in England
Sees, some morning, unaware,
That the lowest boughs and the brushwood sheaf
Round the elm-tree bole are in tiny leaf,
While the chaffinch sings on the orchard bough
In England – now!

Robert Browning

How Do I Love Thee?

How do I love thee? Let me count the ways.
I love thee to the depth and breadth and height
My soul can reach, when feeling out of sight
For the ends of Being and ideal Grace.
I love thee to the level of every day's
Most quiet need, by sun and candle-light.
I love thee freely, as men strive for right;
I love thee purely, as they turn from praise.
I love thee with the passion put to use
In my old griefs, and with my childhood's faith.

I love thee with a love I seemed to lose
With my lost saints – I love thee with the breadth,
Smiles, tears, of all my life! – and if God choose,
I shall but love thee better after death.

Elizabeth Barrett Browning

Compare your parody with other parodies of the same poem written in your group. Do they differ simply because of the ideas expressed or are other elements to be taken into account? You can then, if you wish, read the following parodies of the three poems.

Nursery Rhyme

What are the suburbs made of?
Fridges and freezers and eyebrow tweezers –
that's what the suburbs are made of!

What are the fine houses made of?
Clusters and clarets and 24-carats –
that's what fine houses are made of!

What are the tenements made of?
Dry rot and dampness, congestion and crampness –
That's what the tenements are made of!

Gavin Ewart

Home Truths From Abroad

Oh, to be in England
Now that April's there,
And whoever wakes in England
Sees some morning, in despair,
There's a horrible fog i' the heart o' the town,
And the greasy pavement is damp and brown;
While the rain-drop falls from the laden bough,
In England – now!

Anonymous

Sonnet

How do I hate you? Let me count the ways;
I hate your greying hair, now almost white,
Your blotchy skin, a most repellent sight,
The eyes that stare back in a sort of daze,
The turned-up nose, the hollow that betrays
The missing dentures, taken out at night,
Receding chin, whose colour isn't quite
Masked by the scraggy beard – in a phrase,
I hate the sight of you, as every morn,
We meet each other in our favourite place,
And casually, as to the matter born,
You make your all too customary grimace,
Something between disgust, boredom and scorn;
God, how I loathe you, shaving-mirror face.

Stanley J. Sharpless

B.4.2 Parodying prose

1 Read the following short story by James Thurber and complete the diagram that follows to show who sleeps where and what their sleeping habits are.

B.4

The Night the Bed Fell

I suppose that the high-water mark of my youth in Columbus, Ohio, was the night the bed fell on my father. … It happened, then, that my father had decided to sleep in the attic one night, to be away where he could think. My mother opposed the notion strongly because, she said, the old wooden bed up there was unsafe: it was wobbly and the heavy headboard would crash down on father's head in case the bed fell, and kill him. There was no dissuading him, however, and at a quarter past ten he closed the attic door behind him and went up the narrow twisting stairs. We later heard ominous creakings as he crawled into bed. …

We had visiting us at this time a nervous first cousin of mine named Briggs Beall, who believed that he was likely to cease breathing when he was asleep. It was his feeling that if he were not awakened every hour during the night, he might die of suffocation. He had been accustomed to setting an alarm clock to ring at intervals until morning, but I persuaded him to abandon this. He slept in my room and I told him that I was such a light sleeper that if anybody quit breathing in the same room with me, I would wake instantly. He tested me the first night – which I had suspected he would – by holding his breath after my regular breathing had convinced him I was asleep. I was not asleep, however, and called to him. This seemed to allay his fears a little, but he took the precaution of putting a glass of spirits of camphor on a little table at the head of his bed. In case I didn't arouse him until he was almost gone, he said, he would sniff the camphor, a powerful reviver. …

By midnight we were all in bed. The layout of the rooms and the disposition of their occupants is important to an understanding of what later occurred. In the front room upstairs (just under father's attic bedroom) were my mother and my brother Herman, who sometimes sang in his sleep, usually 'Marching Through Georgia' or 'Onward, Christian Soldiers.' Briggs Beall and myself were in a room adjoining this one. My brother Roy was in a room across the hall from ours. Our bull terrier, Rex, slept in the hall.

My bed was an army cot, one of those affairs which are made wide enough to sleep on comfortably only by putting up, flat with the middle section, the two sides which ordinarily hang down like the sideboards of a drop-leaf table. When these sides are up, it is perilous to roll too far toward the edge, for then the cot is likely to tip completely over, bringing the whole bed down on top of one, with a tremendous banging crash. This, in fact, is precisely what happened, about two o'clock in the morning. (It was my mother who, in recalling the scene later, first referred to it as 'the night the bed fell on your father'.)

Always a deep sleeper, slow to arouse (I had lied to Briggs), I was at first unconscious of what had happened when the iron cot rolled me onto the floor and toppled over on me. It left me still warmly bundled up and unhurt, for the bed rested above me like a canopy. Hence I did not wake up, only reached the edge of consciousness and went back. The racket, however, instantly awakened my mother, in the next room, who came to the immediate conclusion that her worst dread was realized: the big wooden bed upstairs had fallen on father. She therefore screamed, 'Let's go to your poor father!' It was this shout, rather than the noise of my cot falling, that awakened Herman, in the same room with her. He thought that mother had become, for no apparent reason, hysterical. 'You're all right, Mamma!' he shouted, trying to calm her. They exchanged shout for shout for perhaps ten seconds: 'Let's go to your poor father!' and 'You're all right!' That woke up Briggs. By this time I was conscious of what was going on, in a vague way, but did not yet realize that I was under my bed instead of on it. Briggs, awakening in the midst of loud shouts of fear and apprehension, came to the quick conclusion that he was suffocating and that we were all trying to 'bring him out.' With a low moan, he grasped the glass of camphor at the head of his bed and instead of sniffing it poured it over himself. The room reeked of camphor. 'Ugf, ahfg,' choked Briggs, like a drowning man, for he had almost succeeded in stopping his breath under the deluge of pungent spirits. He leaped out of bed and groped toward the open window, but he came up against one that was closed. With his hand, he beat out the glass, and I could hear it crash and tinkle on the alleyway below. It was at this juncture that I, in trying to get up, had the uncanny sensation of feeling my bed above me! Foggy with sleep, I now suspected, in my turn, that the whole uproar was being made in a frantic endeavour to extricate me from what must be an unheard-of and perilous situation. 'Get me out of this!' I bawled. 'Get me out!' I think I had the nightmarish belief that I was entombed in a mine. 'Gugh,' gasped Briggs, floundering in his camphor.

By this time my mother, still shouting, pursued by Herman, still shouting, was trying to open the door to the attic, in order to go up and get my father's body out of the wreckage. The door was stuck, however, and wouldn't yield. Her frantic pulls on it only added to the general banging and confusion. Roy and the dog were now up, the one shouting questions, the other barking.

Father, farthest away and soundest sleeper of all, had by this time been awakened by the battering on the attic door. He decided that the house was on fire. 'I'm coming, I'm coming!' he wailed in a slow, sleepy voice – it took him many minutes to regain full consciousness. My mother, still believing he was caught under the bed, detected in his 'I'm coming!' the mournful, resigned note of one who is preparing to meet his Maker. 'He's dying!' she shouted.

'I'm all right!' Briggs yelled to reassure her. 'I'm all right!' He still believed that it was his own closeness to death that was worrying mother. I found at last the light switch in my room, unlocked the door, and Briggs and I joined the others at the attic door. The dog, who never did like Briggs, jumped for him – assuming that he was the culprit in whatever was going on – and Roy had to throw Rex and hold him. We could hear father crawling out of bed upstairs. Roy pulled the attic door open, with a mighty jerk, and father came down the stairs, sleepy and irritable but safe and sound. My mother began to weep when she saw him. Rex began to howl. "What in the name of God is going on here?' asked father.

The situation was finally put together like a gigantic jigsaw puzzle. Father caught a cold prowling around in his bare feet but there were no other bad results. 'I'm glad', said mother, who always looked on the bright side of things, 'that your grandfather wasn't here.'

(From James Thurber, *My Life and Hard Times*)

Now, using arrows, show how the chain of events moves from one character to the next. The first arrow has been marked '1' on the diagram.

B.4

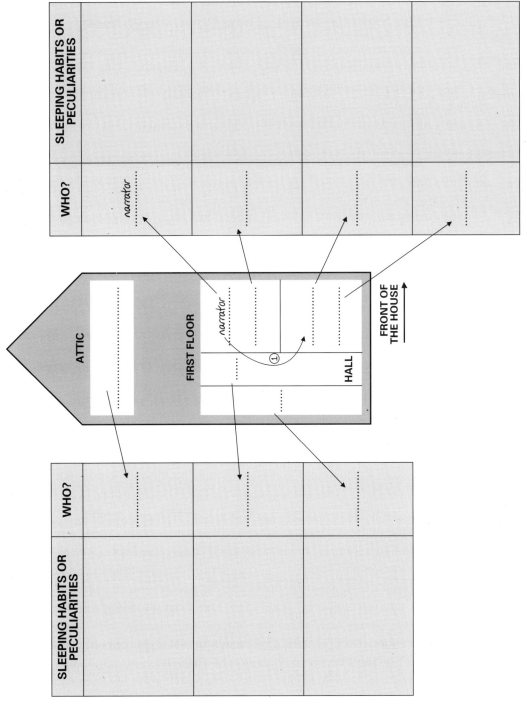

SLEEPING HABITS OR PECULIARITIES

WHO?

narrator

ATTIC

FIRST FLOOR

narrator

①

HALL

FRONT OF
THE HOUSE

WHO?

SLEEPING HABITS OR PECULIARITIES

2 Here is an excerpt from a parody of Thurber's story by Alex Atkinson.

B.4

The Night the Buffalo Came Down the Chimney

… I slept in a hammock in the box-room. One end of this hammock was screwed to the mantelpiece and the other end was nailed to the wall. Whenever anyone banged on the wall the nail, which was loose, came out, and I fell face downward into a zinc bath full of water which Great-aunt Emilia kept in the box-room for emergencies. She lived in constant dread of emergencies, as did most of my family; and the emergency she chiefly feared was a failure of the supply of drinking water. The reason I didn't move the bath out of harm's way was that I had already made up my mind to be a writer of humorous pieces. In the next room (a sort of big attic where Great-aunt Emilia's husband had kept his elephant guns and hunting trophies) my brother Roy slept in a native canoe fitted with walnut feet, and Grandfather on an old iron bed. Immediately below them, in the parlour, Uncle Ebenezer K. Fosdyke (whose colored maid could make a noise like a flock of wild ducks) was accommodated on a chaise-longue, with tablecloths for bedclothes. Uncle Ebenezer was shortsighted. The bedrooms were on the ground floor, and for a very good reason. Great-aunt Emilia reasoned that if the water supply gave out, or if the ghost of her cousin Rufus took it into his head to start prowling around (as he sometimes did), it would be handy to leap straight out of bed, through the window, and on to East Vallet Street. That way you wouldn't have to fight your way downstairs, riddled with cholera or chased by cousin Rufus, and try to get out the front door. There was sense in this, for nobody had been able to open the front door since 1896, when it stuck. As for the back door, Aunt Emilia padlocked it every night and hid the key in the works of an old grandfather clock which lay on its side in the box-room.

My mother and Great-aunt Emilia slept in the first bedroom. In the second bedroom there were my father and a second cousin called Neb. Cousin Neb had a long red beard, and was of a nervous disposition. He frequently awoke in the dead of night under the firm impression that he was a character out of Macbeth. Sometimes he was several characters at once. 'Macbeth has murdered sleep!' he would shout, thudding wild-eyed into your room in his night-shirt. 'Give me the daggers!' The only cure was to throw warm water in his face. Cold water, for some reason, only made him worse. The third bedroom contained two friends of my grandfather's – Hiram Parmit and his wife Rachel. They were both eighty, and there was something the matter with the way their minds worked: I never found out what it was.

> This was how things stood, then, when at some time shortly after three in the morning Uncle Ebenezer's colored maid, Rebecca, came right across town to tell him she had felt the foundations of the house shake under her.

What is the main technique used by Alex Atkinson to parody Thurber's *The Night the Bed Fell*? List several examples to justify your view, then discuss the parody with the rest of the group. Do you all agree on the technique used?

3 This is only the beginning of the parody. Write a further paragraph.

4 Now write your own parody. Choose an author or a work you know well and, if possible, one that has marked stylistic features. List these features: are they syntactic or lexical? Or do they relate to the ideas and contents of the text?

Decide how you will parody the work:

- by exaggerating the writer's style?
- by imitating the style but by using an unusual or ludicrous subject?
- by other means?

Write your parody, then show it to a friend or the rest of the group. Can they recognize what author or work is being parodied?

B.5 Parodying a genre

1 Here is the parody of a recipe:

Rat Soufflé

Make sure that the rat's squeals are not audible from the street, particularly in areas where the Anti-Soufflé League and similar do-gooders are out to persecute the innocent pleasures of the table.

   Anyway, cut the rat down and lay it on the chopping-board. Raise the chopper high above your head, with the steel glinting in the setting sun, and then bring it down – wham! – with a vivid crunch – straight across the taut neck of the terrified rodent, and make it into a soufflé.

(From Monty Python, *The Brand New Monty Python Book*)

Which of these factors makes the text striking?

- the fact that the usual form of a recipe is distorted
- the absurd contents within the traditional form of a recipe
- the distortion of both form and contents

2 A number of epitaphs, often even genuine ones, can be seen as parodies since they use wit and humour and often criticize the dead person instead of praising him or her in a more sober way. For example:

> Here lies the body of Richard Hind,
> Who was neither ingenious, sober, nor kind.
>
> ...
>
> Here was a man who was killed by lightning.
> He died when his prospects seemed to be brightening
> He might have cut a flash in this world of trouble,
> But the flash cut him, and he lies in the stubble.

Some writers have turned such parodies of the epitaph into poems. For example:

Epitaph on a Tyrant

Perfection, of a kind, was what he was after,
And the poetry he invented was easy to understand;
He knew human folly like the back of his hand,
And was greatly interested in armies and fleets;
When he laughed, respectable senators burst with laughter,
And when he cried the little children died in the streets.

W. H. Auden

(You could also read Auden's 'The Unknown Citizen'.)

How would you describe each of these epitaphs? (As amusing / critical / cynical / etc.)

3 Working in pairs or small groups, choose a person (alive or dead) whose epitaph you would like to write. Then list all the characteristics you wish to mention. Remember that you are writing a parody of an epitaph, and that you therefore need to think of humorous, negative and probably exaggerated personality traits. Then write your epitaph, in prose or verse, making sure that you respect the rules of composition of this type of text:

Here lies ... + *Who was ...* / *Who* + verb
or
He/She died ... / *He/She* + verb ...
Do not mention the name of the person.

Exchange your epitaphs. Can you guess whose epitaphs the other groups have written? Can you make any suggestions to improve their style or contents?

4 Write another parody of a recipe or epitaph, or do the same with another genre. For example, an extract from:

a soap opera	a horoscope
a detective story	a tourist brochure
an instruction manual	a formal letter
a dictionary	an obituary
a travel book written	a language-teaching book
by one person	a science fiction story
a romantic novel	a cover blurb

B.5

Part C **Variations on a theme**

As a rule, the sign that a beginner has a genuine original talent is that he is more interested in playing with words than in saying something original ...

(W H. Auden, *The Dyer's Hand and Other Essays*)

One way of playing with language is to consider the enormous differences that can be made to a text by changing a number of variables such as bias, genre, stylistic features or narrative techniques. Starting with similar facts or ideas, you can end up with extremely diverse texts.

In this section you are encouraged to play and experiment with such variables and to compare and study the resulting texts.

C.1 Bias

A biased article does not present the information in a fair and objective way; the exposition of the facts is influenced by personal or political opinion; the statements are coloured to defend certain points of view. This is not to be confused with an opinion column in which the journalist openly defends a view.

Bias mostly appears through:

- the choice of **pictures**, which can influence the reader before he or she even starts the article. Compare, for instance, these two pictures of Sir Edward Heath (a former Conservative Prime Minister) which appeared on the same day in the *Daily Express* and the *Daily Mirror*, on the occasion of his being made a Knight of the Garter[1]:

DELIGHTED: Sir Edward outside his Salisbury home yesterday

HONOURED: Heath

[1]Knight of the Garter: a civil decoration.

Which one do you think appeared in the *Daily Express* (Conservative)? And which in the *Daily Mirror* (Labour)?

- the **amount of space** devoted to the article;

- a clearly expressed point of view in the **subhead** or the **lead-in**, to make sure that the reader will get the point even if he or she does not read the whole article. The article about Sir Edward Heath in the *Daily Express*, for instance, had two subheads:

'Rare honour by the Queen makes ex-Premier a Knight of the Garter'; 'Veteran MP Heath's joy over royal accolade'.

What words show the journalist's bias in these two subheads?

- the **choice of information** reported. Statistics, for example, can be treated in very different ways depending on what you want to prove;

- **vague statements**, whose source is not mentioned (e.g. *It was reported that ... / Officials said ... / One expert said last night ... / Experts warned ...*);

- the **language** used, particularly:
    - colloquial expressions, partly to create a feeling of complicity between the journalist and the reader, and partly because such expressions usually convey strong emotions. For example, *put up with* instead of *tolerate*.
    - strong or exaggerated language. For example, *in chaos* rather than *disorganized*.

Can you underline the words or expressions showing bias in the following sentences?

'Labour was on course for an embarrassing own goal last night in a Commons vote on the Budget.' *(Daily Mail)*

'Tory Councillors have started a £11,000 town hall "lottery" in a desperate bid to get this year's poll tax rolling in. The names of people who pay the hated charge on time will be entered in a big prize draw.' *(Daily Mirror)*

1 Read and compare the following two articles. In the chart on page 77, list
the reasons why you find one more biased than the other.

BOTTOM OF THE CLASS

Only Brazil, Mozambique and the old Soviet Union have WORSE schools

SHOCK END OF TERM REPORT

By RICHARD GARNER

OUR schools are the pits, a shock survey reveals today.

Secondary schools are so short of books that only Brazil, Mozambique and the old Soviet Union can claim to be worse off in the world.

Primary schools really hit rock bottom on book shortages AND come just one from bottom on oversized classes.

The shameful figures – from the highly-respected National Foundation for Educational Research – cover secondary schools in 20 countries and primary schools in 14.

Nations like Korea and Taiwan come out on top.

Even Slovenia, which wasn't even an independent country when John Major became Prime Minister, has fewer schools with book shortages than England and Wales.

In both our primary and secondary schools, 31 per cent complained of science and maths book shortages.

And 57 per cent of primary schools warned of oversized classrooms.

The findings sparked off a storm yesterday, with teachers and Labour party chiefs pinning the blame on 13 years of Tory cuts.

Labour's education spokesman Jack Straw said: 'This is a damning indictment of Tory neglect and a national humiliation.'

Warning

'We will tackle the scandal of Britain's crumbling schools. We shall outlaw oversized classrooms and give children the books they need.'

Doug McAvoy, general secretary of the 181,000-strong National Union of Teachers, added: 'We've been warning the Government of the damage caused by oversized classes and shortages of books.

'It's refused to admit it. Now we're bottom of the pile.'

The crisis is at its worst in Tory Education Secretary Kenneth Clarke's own constituency of Rushcliffe in Nottingham. A hard-up comprehensive school is begging parents for more than £100 a year each to bail it out.

PRIMARY SCHOOLS WITH OVERCROWDED CLASSROOMS	
1 Portugal	(15%)
2 Taiwan	(15%)
3 Italy	(24%)
4 United States	(27%)
5 Hungary	(29%)
6 Spain	(31%)
7 Canada	(35%)
8 Scotland and Korea	(41%)
10 Ireland	(46%)
11 Slovenia	(48%)
12 Israel	(50%)
13 ENGLAND	(57%)
14 Soviet Union	(80%)

PRIMARY SCHOOLS WITH BOOK SHORTAGES	
1 Korea and Taiwan	(1%)
3 United Kingdom	(3%)
4 Hungary	(6%)
5 Canada and Israel	(9%)
7 Italy and Portugal	(10%)
9 Spain	(12%)
10 Slovenia	(16%)
11 Ireland	(17%)
12 Scotland	(19%)
13 Soviet Union	(24%)
14 ENGLAND	(31%)

SECONDARY SCHOOLS WITH BOOK SHORTAGES	
1 Taiwan	(0%)
2 Korea	(1%)
3 Italy	(2%)
4 France and China	(4%)
6 Switzerland and Hungary	(6%)
8 United States	(7%)
9 Spain	(10%)
10 Slovenia, Canada, Israel and Jordan	(13%)
14 Ireland	(14%)
15 Portugal	(22%)
16 Scotland	(24%)
17 ENGLAND	(31%)
18 Soviet Union	(32%)
19 Brazil	(43%)
20 Mozambique	(85%)

(From the *Daily Mirror*, 13 March 1992)

World's best leave British children trailing in science

THE PERFORMANCE of British pupils in mathematics and science is way behind that of children in South Korea and Taiwan, according to tests in 20 countries.

The second International Assessment of International Progress suggests that Britain's performance – which is around the international average – may be linked with too little maths and science homework, too many streamed classes, and a particularly poor performance among the least able pupils. The top 5 per cent in England and Scotland are world leaders, but the least able 50 per cent of children trail their international counterparts. Thousands of children were set identical questions on maths and science topics during 1990. Nine-year-olds in South Korea led the field in maths by a large margin – scoring 75 per cent.

The next best performers were Taiwan, Hungary and Italy, all on 68 per cent. England (59 per cent) came eleventh out of the 14 countries that tested nine-year-olds, with Scotland fourth (66 per cent) and Ireland ninth (60 per cent).

At 13, China headed the maths league, with a score of 80 per cent, and Korea and Taiwan jointly second, on 73 per cent. England, Scotland and Ireland all landed in the middle, scoring 61 per cent.

Korean children topped the table in science at both 9 and 13, with scores of 68 and 78 per cent respectively. Taiwan again took second place, with English children appearing in the middle of the international league. Hungarian children came out fourth overall, with Swiss 13-year-olds leading the western European nations. Neither Japan nor Germany took part. Italian children performed slightly better than the English; French children much the same.

The results found no necessary link between class sizes and performance. South Korean schools, which consistently led the international league, have an average class size of 49 pupils for 13-year-olds and one-third of Korean classes for nine-year-olds had more than 45 pupils. That contrasts with England, where 73 per cent of schools have class sizes between 26 and 35 for nine-year-olds – comparatively large, by international standards. In the United States, an even weaker performer than England, no class of nine-year-olds has more than 35 pupils.

Similarly, there was no firm link between performance and the use of calculators: Korean children rarely use calculators, particularly younger children, whereas nearly all British 13-year-olds use them in school.

But homework was a clear success factor. The volume of science and maths homework given to English and Scots children was lower than in any of the other countries: half of English nine-year-olds said they received no science or maths homework from their teachers. By contrast, one-third of Korean children said they did more than four hours' maths homework a week.

However, there was some indication that English and Scots children would have performed better in tests that leant more strongly towards scientific experiments, because they spend more time on that kind of work than children in other countries. English children were particularly weak on arithmetic, which counted quite heavily in the tests, and algebra. But they performed better than average at geometry, and data analysis.

Across the globe, boys scored higher results in both maths and science (particularly at 13). But girls were not uniformly behind: in England, they performed better than boys on maths problem solving and around the world (including England) girls were better at interpreting scientific data, formulating hypotheses and deducing results.

(From the *Independent*, 13 March 1992)

	More biased article from	More objective article from ....
Layout		
Information given		
Conclusions drawn from it		
Political bias		
Familiar language		
Biased language		
Other factors		

C.1

2 Look at the two excerpts from articles published on the same day in the *Daily Mail* and in the *Daily Mirror*.

– Which one is an excerpt from an opinion column?
– Which one is an excerpt from a news article?

Labour ignored hospital denial over death of baby in 'dirty tricks' advert

By PAUL HENDERSON

LABOUR went ahead with its advertising campaign blaming NHS cuts for a baby's death even though it knew hospital officials categorically denied the claims, it was revealed yesterday.

The party spent £130,000 on full page adverts in seven national newspapers on Wednesday claiming 18-month-old Georgina Norris, who had a rare heart disease, died through lack of funds.

But Great Ormond Street hospital officials have repeatedly denied the claims for more than three months.

(From the *Daily Mail*, 13 March 1992)

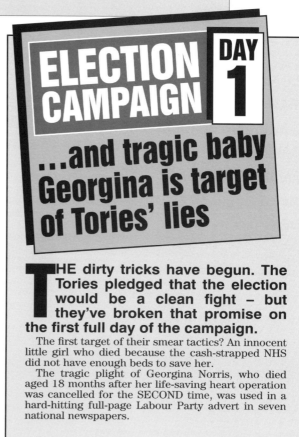

ELECTION CAMPAIGN DAY 1

...and tragic baby Georgina is target of Tories' lies

THE dirty tricks have begun. The Tories pledged that the election would be a clean fight – but they've broken that promise on the first full day of the campaign.

The first target of their smear tactics? An innocent little girl who died because the cash-strapped NHS did not have enough beds to save her.

The tragic plight of Georgina Norris, who died aged 18 months after her life-saving heart operation was cancelled for the SECOND time, was used in a hard-hitting full-page Labour Party advert in seven national newspapers.

(From the *Daily Mirror*, 13 March 1992)

1 List all the features that contribute to the bias of the excerpts.
2 What are the facts about what happened?
3 Write an objective account of what happened, based on these facts.

C.1

3 Transform the following headlines into biased ones. The beginning of each article is given as well to make the context clear.

Now show your headlines to someone else and see whether they can find the bias in each one. If your message is clear you should not have to explain it.

a

Television debate is ruled out by Major

John Major ruled out a televised election debate with Neil Kinnock and Paddy Ashdown yesterday when he told the Commons: 'Every party politician that expects to lose tries that trick, and every politician who expects to win says no.' … Mr Kinnock replied that they should have nothing to fear from the electorate: 'Let's have a debate, let's fix the date, let's get on with it.'

(From the *Independent,* 14 April 1992)

b

Students want fees scrapped at colleges

THE OUTGOING president of the National Union of Students called yesterday for an immediate government commitment to free higher education.

(From *The Times,* 14 April 1992)

c

Building jobs to fall by another 300,000

THE CONSTRUCTION industry is heading for another 300,000 job losses by the end of the year, according to a state-of-trade enquiry by the Building Employers Confederation …

(From *The Times,* 14 April 1992)

d

Free exit

MOTORISTS using the Severn bridge will be charged nothing to leave Wales in two weeks' time while those wishing to return will have to pay £2.80. The rise in charges will be used partly to finance a new £300 million crossing of the river.

(From *The Times,* 14 April 1992)

C.1

4 Read the following two headlines and articles. Transform the headlines into objective ones.

a

Libs blast tax band

The Liberal democrats yesterday joined Labour in opposing chancellor Norman Lamont's 20p tax band.

(From the *Daily Mirror*, 13 March 1992)

b

Blunder in Steph hunt

Two vital days in the hunt for the kidnapper of Stephanie Slater were lost by police because of a computer blunder, it was revealed yesterday.

(From the *Daily Mirror*, 13 April 1992)

C.1

5 Rewrite the following article, making it neutral.

Poor face tax blow

THE poor will suffer under the new council tax, Labour claimed yesterday.

For example in Leicester a couple in a house valued at less than £40,000, would be charged £629 a year – **FOUR TIMES** as much as a family in a £320,000 mansion.

The replacement for the hated poll tax will come in next March. But it is just as unfair, environment spokesman Bryan Gould warned as he launched Labour's local elections campaign.

(From the *Daily Mirror*, 14 April 1992)

6 Expand the following articles, and transform them into biased ones, having first chosen the newspaper or the type of reader you want to write them for.

Benn backs animals

Tony Benn, Labour MP for Chesterfield, yesterday joined Biafran prince Keni St George of Ozo in an animal rights demonstration in London. The singer was conducting a 12-hour vigil in Trafalgar Square with live goats and an 8ft-high Buddha to protest at mistreatment of animals.

(From the *Guardian*, 13 March 1992)

Traffic growth

Motor traffic in 1991 was 3 per cent higher than in 1990, according to provisional figures from the Department of Transport. Cars increased by 4 per cent, but light vans fell by 2 per cent and heavy goods vehicles by 3 per cent.

(From the *Independent*, 13 March 1992)

Suspended MP to stand

John Browne, the MP suspended from the Commons for failing to declare business interests, yesterday announced he would stand against the official Tory candidate in his Winchester constituency.

(From the *Guardian*, 13 March 1992)

C. 1

C.2 The implied reader

Whether you are writing an essay, a report, a letter or an article, you have to think of your potential readers, of their needs and expectations.

1 Compare, for example, these two paragraphs about the English poet William Blake:

a   William Blake, a poet and an artist, illustrated the works of Young, Blair, Gray and others. Much of his poetry has hidden meanings that are hard to understand. He did not believe in the reality of matter, or in the power of earthly rulers, or in punishment after death. His best known works include *Songs of Innocence* (1787) and *Songs of Experience* (1794). The second is darker and heavier than the first; but it does contain some good poems.

(From G. C. Thornley, *An Outline of English Literature*)

b   Most of what currently passes for movements of human liberation would have been condemned by Blake as what he bitterly called Druidism, taking the name from what he judged to have been the native British version of natural religion. All of Blake's work is based on a firm distinction between what is imaginative and what is merely natural in us, with the natural rejected, cast out beyond the balance of what Blake termed 'contraries'. The revolt of youth-as-youth Blake saw as a cyclic self-defeat, the sad destiny of the eternal rebel he called Orc. The revolt of women-as-women (as exemplified in his acquaintance Mary Wollstonecraft) he judged also as doomed to the perpetual failure of natural cycle, for all natural women, like all natural men, were subject to what he named the Female Will, always rampant in nature. The revolt of the heart against the head (as represented by Rousseau) he pungently characterized as 'reasoning from the loins in the unreal forms of Beulah's Night', Beulah being a lower paradise of illusory appearances.

(From Bloom & Trilling, *The Oxford Anthology of English Literature*)

Both of these excerpts come from textbooks, but it is clear that they were written for very different kinds of students of literature. What kind of student do you think each passage was written for?

Complete the following table with examples to show the tendency towards simplification or generalization in one text and towards more complexity and subtlety in the other.

	Passage a	Passage b
Vocabulary		
Syntax		
Literary / historical references		
Ideas discussed		

2 Any writer thus starts by asking him- or herself 'Who am I writing for?' Even novelists and poets usually have an implied reader in mind. Some of the questions you should ask yourself are the following:

– Who will my readers be? The general public? A specialized group of people (e.g. students at a given level; engineers; people practising a certain sport)?
– How much do you think they know about the subject you are writing about? Nothing at all? A little? Or are they specialists in it?
– What are their expectations? Are you writing to entertain them, to show them a slightly different aspect of a field they are familiar with, or will all that you write be new to them?

C.2

In the activity that follows you are asked to work as a whole group on a subject that you all know well. So you can start by taking your school or university as a theme. You should each write a short text (150–300 words) to present the school or one aspect of the school. But you must do so with a specific kind of reader in mind. For example:

– a foreign student who knows nothing about the educational system in your country;
– a group of teachers who work in a similar school nearby but need to know what is specific to *your* school;
– an architect who needs to know how the buildings can be improved;
– an institution which has asked to rent the school and its facilities during the summer;
– other.

When you have finished, exchange your text with a partner and see if you can guess the reader for whom their text has been written.

Can any of the questions in the list above help you to improve your text?

C.3 Point of view and narrative technique

1 Look at the picture below and try to understand what is happening. Answer the following questions, but do not write anything yet.

   1 Why is the couple coming through the door in fancy dress?
   2 Have they made a mistake? Why? Or are they doing it on purpose? If so, why?
   3 What happened before this scene?
   4 What will take place afterwards?
   5 What were people talking about before the arrival of the couple?
   6 What will they say afterwards?

Johnnie Walker's guide to success.

You will soon be asked to write an account of this scene, but before doing so read (a) and (b) below and decide what point of view and what narrative technique you wish to adopt.

a Remember that the **point of view** relates to **who** tells the story. Will your story be told:

– in the first person?
– in the third person?

If it is told in the third person, will you choose:

– an omniscient narrator, who, like a god, can go in and out of the characters' minds, and who sees and knows everything?
– the more limited vision of one character, whose thoughts and actions we follow without being conscious of a narrator? If so, what character will you choose as 'central intelligence': the major character (for example the man in fancy dress in the picture) or a minor one?

b **Narrative technique** relates to **the way** the story is told, to how words and actions are reported. Imagine that the man in fancy dress says 'Sorry we're late!'. You can report this in several ways:

(i)   narration: *He came in and apologized for being late.*
(ii)   indirect speech: *He said he was sorry that he was late.*
(iii) free indirect speech: *He was sorry he was late.*
(iv)   direct speech: *'Sorry we're late,' the man said.*
(v)   free direct speech: *'Sorry we're late!'*

In the narrative techniques close to (i) the narrator appears to be more clearly in control of his report. As you move towards (v), on the other hand, you increasingly get the feeling that the narrator is standing back and letting the characters reveal themselves directly.

Now relate the scene in the picture, choosing a point of view and a way of reporting the words and actions of the characters. You can choose to relate a very brief scene (the few minutes before and after the picture was taken) or a longer story, including what happened further back in the past and what happens afterwards.

Compare the different stories produced in your group. Which points of view and narrative techniques – or combination of both – produce the most striking or interesting effects? Why?

2 Choose another point of view and narrative technique and write a short text based on the following paintings by the surrealist painter Magritte and by the eighteenth-century English painter Gainsborough.

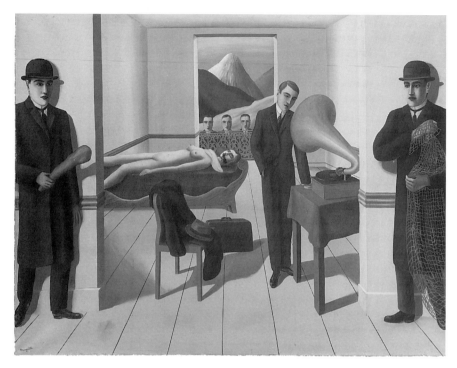

Magritte, René. *The Menaced Assassin (L'Assassin menacé)*. (1926). Oil on canvas, 59¼" × 6' 4⅞" (150.4 × 195.2 cm). The Museum of Modern Art, New York. Kay Sage Tanguy Fund. Photograph © 1996 The Museum of Modern Art, New York.

Thomas Gainsborough, *Mr and Mrs Robert Andrews*. (Reproduced by courtesy of the Trustees, The National Gallery, London.)

Then read your text to the others in your group, or exchange texts. For each of the new texts you hear or read can you tell:

- if the narrator is an omniscient one?
- if the scene is seen through the eyes of one character, and if so, which one?
- how the words or actions are reported?

Discuss any problem or inconsistency within your group.

3 Read this brief summary of the short story *Tobermory* by Saki.

'Tobermory' recounts a disconcerting incident at Lady Blemley's house-party. ... Mr Appin, most unprepossessing and unpromising of house-guests, announces to the astonishment of all that he has discovered how to teach animals to talk and that his first successful pupil has been none other than Lady Blemley's pet cat Tobermory. At which point, Tobermory enters the room. Constraint becomes panic when it is apparent from his replies to questions that Tobermory is a cat that enjoys telling home-truths.

(From Walter Allen, *The Short Story in English*)

Write the short story, choosing:

- the point of view (one of the guests? Lady Blemley's? Tobermory's? etc.);
- the type of narration;
- the anecdote(s) related by the cat.

C.3

Then compare your stories and study the effects produced by the different approaches chosen.

C.4 Different genres

C.4.1 Choosing a genre

Choose one of the following two photographs and draft a short passage about it or related to it. The text you write should belong to a given genre. For example:

a small ad
instructions
a postcard
a letter
a passage from a detective story
a passage from an essay
a passage from a play
a passage from a psychological novel
a passage from a diary
a poem
a proverb
a travel brochure

Wright Morris,
Church and House,
Virginia City, 1941

Wright Morris,
Faulkner Country,
near Oxford,
Mississippi, 1940

Exchange texts with the other members of your group. With each text decide:

- which photograph it refers to;
- which genre it belongs to.

If necessary, make suggestions about how to improve the language, structure, layout or contents to make it more typical of its genre.

Then give the texts back and write the final version of your own text.

C.4.2 Turning one genre into another

1 Read the beginning of the play *An Inspector Calls* by J. B. Priestley on pages 90–91. Then complete the family tree below with the names of the characters.

ACT ONE

The dining-room of a fairly large suburban house, belonging to a prosperous manufacturer. It has good solid furniture of the period. The general effect is substantial and heavily comfortable, but not cosy and homelike. …

At rise of curtain, the four BIRLINGS *and* GERALD *are seated at the table, with* ARTHUR BIRLING *at one end, his wife at the other,* ERIC *downstage, and* SHEILA *and* GERALD *seated upstage.* EDNA, *the parlour-maid, is just clearing the table, which has no cloth, of dessert plates and champagne glasses, etc., and then replacing them with decanter of port, cigar box and cigarettes. Port glasses are already on the table. All five are in evening dress of the period, the men in tails and white ties, not dinner-jackets.* ARTHUR BIRLING *is a heavy-looking, rather portentous man in his middle fifties with fairly easy manners but rather provincial in his speech. His wife is about fifty, a rather cold woman and her husband's social superior.* SHEILA *is a pretty girl in her early twenties, very pleased with life and rather excited.* GERALD CROFT *is an attractive chap about thirty, rather too manly to be a dandy but very much the easy well-bred young man-about-town.* ERIC *is in his early twenties, not quite at ease, half shy, half assertive. At the moment they have all had a good dinner, are celebrating a special occasion, and are pleased with themselves.*

BIRLING: Giving us the port, Edna? That's right. [*He pushes it towards* ERIC.] You ought to like this port, Gerald. As a matter of fact, Finchley told me it's exactly the same port your father gets from him.

GERALD: Then it'll be all right. The governor prides himself on being a good judge of port. I don't pretend to know much about it.

SHEILA [*gaily, possessively*]: I should jolly well think not, Gerald. I'd hate you to know all about port – like one of these purple-faced old men.

BIRLING: Here, I'm not a purple-faced old man.

SHEILA: No, not yet. But then you don't know all about port – do you?

BIRLING [*noticing that his wife has not taken any*]: Now then, Sybil, you must take a little tonight. Special occasion, y'know, eh?

SHEILA: Yes, go on, Mummy. You must drink our health.

MRS BIRLING [*smiling*]: Very well, then. Just a little, thank you. [*To* EDNA, *who is about to go, with tray*] All right, Edna. I'll ring from the drawing-room when we want coffee. Probably in about half an hour.

EDNA [*going*]: Yes, ma'am.

[EDNA *goes out. They now have all the glasses filled.* BIRLING *beams at them and clearly relaxes.*]

BIRLING: Well, well – this is very nice. Very nice. Good dinner too, Sybil. Tell Cook from me.

GERALD [*politely*]: Absolutely first-class.

MRS BIRLING [*reproachfully:*] Arthur, you're not supposed to say such things –

BIRLING: Oh – come, come – I'm treating Gerald like one of the family. And I'm sure he won't object.

SHEILA [*with mock aggressiveness*]: Go on, Gerald – just you object!

GERALD [*smiling*]: Wouldn't dream of it. In fact, I insist upon being one of the family now. I've been trying long enough, haven't I? [*As she does not reply, with more insistence*] Haven't I? You know I have.

MRS BIRLING [*smiling*]: Of course she does.

SHEILA [*half serious, half playful*]: Yes – except for all last summer, when you never came near me, and I wondered what had happened to you.

GERALD: And I've told you – I was awfully busy at the works all that time.

SHEILA [*same tone as before*]: Yes, that's what *you* say.

MRS BIRLING: Now, Sheila, don't tease him. When you're married you'll realize that men with important work to do sometimes have to spend nearly all their time and energy on their business. You'll have to get used to that, just as I had.

(From J. B. Priestley, *An Inspector Calls*)

C.4

2 What is the family celebrating?
3 Underline all the details that show:

– that the family is well-off;
– that they are feeling pleased with themselves.

Which is the only remark that brings a darker note to the occasion?

You can then read or act out the scene in groups of five students.

2 Rewrite the passage in order to make it into the beginning of a short story or novel. Remember that you can:

– report the words directly or indirectly, using a variety of verbs;
– report all the words or only those that seem most significant to you, using summaries or narrative for the rest of the text;
– add any description or explanation you feel is needed to set the scene.

Do not forget to choose a point of view (see page 84).

Then compare and discuss your different versions.

3 Many novels are adapted for the stage, cinema or television. Read the beginning of a novel by Alison Lurie given below and then transform it into the start of a stage play or television drama. Include as many stage directions as you consider necessary, without forgetting the introductory ones which describe the setting and the characters at the beginning of a play. Add lines of dialogue if you want to.

Chapter 1

The day on which Emily Stockwell Turner fell out of love with her husband began much like other days. As usual, Emmy lay in bed twenty minutes later than she should have done, with her son Freddy playing cars over her legs, and when she finally got up it seemed as if things would never be sorted out. But somehow breakfast was made; Freddy was fed and dressed and sent off to nursery school in the car pool, and at length Emmy stood outside the house watching her husband leave for work on time.

'Looks like snow,' said Turner, an instructor in the Languages and Literature Division at Convers College, as he stood beside her on the frozen lawn in his overcoat. It was a chilly, dark morning early in November, and Emmy wore only an old cashmere sweater and slacks, but she was the kind that never feels the cold.

'Oh, good; do you think so? But it's only the first week in November. I'm afraid it's much too soon.'

'It probably snows early here,' Holman said, and climbed into his car and shut the door. Through the glass he could see Emmy look round at the clouds, smiling. What a magnificent creature she is, he thought, as he frequently did. She was a big girl, tall, tanned like a gypsy, and with a high colour. Her heavy, bright-brown hair had not yet been done up for the day; it hung down over one shoulder in a thick braid. She was twenty-seven, and still had, as on the day he married her, the look of a carefully bred and beautifully groomed animal kept permanently at the peak of its condition for some high use which has not yet arrived and possibly never will arrive. Holman had seen it often on boys and girls of Emmy's class, though seldom to such a degree or accompanied by so much beauty.

Emmy continued to stand beside the car, waiting for her husband to roll the window down, so he rolled it down.

'Goodbye, darling,' she said, stooping to kiss him.

'So long, baby,' Holman replied. He rolled the window up again and drove away down the drive.

Emmy stood on the lawn, smiling, and watching his car, a little grey Volkswagen, turn into the road and grow smaller as it went away from her along the highway, between low hills covered with scrub pines and birches.

(From Alison Lurie, *Love and Friendship*)

Compare and discuss your different versions. Then perform some of them.

C.5 Illustrating parables and proverbs

1 A parable is a story about everyday events which is told in order to make a moral or religious point. In the Bible, Jesus often conveys his message through parables. Read the following parable from the New Testament. The King James, or 'Authorized' Version (1611) is given first; a modern translation follows afterwards.

---

16 And he spake a parable unto them, saying, The ground of a certain rich man brought forth plentifully:

17 And he thought within himself, saying, What shall I do, because I have no room where to bestow my fruits?

18 And he said, This will I do: I will pull down my barns, and build greater; and there will I bestow all my fruits and my goods. *19* And I will say to my soul, Soul, thou hast much goods laid up for many years; take thine ease, eat, drink, *and* be merry. *20* But God said unto him, *Thou* fool, this night thy soul shall be required of thee: then whose shall those things be, which thou hast provided? *21* So *is* he that layeth up treasure for himself, and is not rich toward God.

(Luke 12. 16–21)

Then Jesus told them this parable: 'There was once a rich man who had land which bore good crops. He began to think to himself, 'I haven't anywhere to keep all my crops. What can I do?' 'This is what I will do,' he told himself. 'I will tear down my barns and build bigger ones, where I will store my corn and all my other goods. Then I will say to myself, Lucky man! You have all the good things you need for many years. Take life easy, eat, drink, and enjoy yourself!' But God said to him, 'You fool! This very night you will have to give up your life; then who will get all these things you have kept for yourself?'

And Jesus concluded, 'This is how it is with those who pile up riches for themselves but are not rich in God's sight.'

(From the *Good News Bible*, 1976)

What do you think is the message of this parable?

- One should not make plans for the future since unexpected things may take place.
- One should think of one's soul before thinking of one's comfort.
- It is wrong to be too rich.
- Everyone has to die, therefore one should think about it beforehand.
- Other.

Do you all agree?

2 Working in pairs or small groups, discuss what the parable means today. Do you know anyone around you, or any public figure, who resembles the rich man in the parable? If not, can you think of characters or situations which are similar in your society? Then write a modern version of this parable. Don't forget to keep the message the same, even though you change the characters and the setting.

Now compare your different versions of the parable.

3 Write a modern version of another parable or fable. Here are a few possibilities, but there are of course many others.

The good Samaritan (Luke 10)
The merciless servant (Matthew 18)
The sower (Matthew 13)

The hare and the tortoise
The ant and the grasshopper
The fox and the grapes

C.5

Then exchange stories with other students and try to identify the parables or fables which they illustrate.

4 Now do the same thing with proverbs. Choose one (see page 39 for some examples) and write a modern story to convey its message.

When you have finished, exchange stories and try to guess what proverb each one illustrates.

C.6 Stylistic constraints

The following exercise should help you to play with language and to avoid some of the clichés that too often come to mind. Adjectives and adverbs, for instance, are frequently weak and unnecessary and rarely have a truly original or evocative effect (e.g. a cliché such as 'dark night'). Trying to write a text *without* adjectives is therefore a good way of avoiding mechanical formulas and expressions.

1 Describe the following painting or write a short essay or poem about it, respecting one of the following stylistic constraints:

- do not use any adjectives;
- do not use any adverbs;
- do not use any relative clauses;
- use as many modal auxiliaries as possible;
- use an 'unusual tense' as much as possible, for example the conditional perfect, the future perfect. (Your use of the tense will of course have to be justified.)

You can choose the narrator and the point of view you like.

Wyeth, Andrew. *Christina's World.* (1948). Tempera on gessoed panel,32¼ × 47¾" (81.9 × 121.3 cm). The Museum of Modern Art, New York. Purchase. Photograph © 1996 The Museum of Modern Art, New York.

C.5

When you have finished, exchange your text with those of other students and see if you can find out what constraints have been imposed on *their* texts. What stylistic effects are created by such constraints? Which did you find most interesting and why?

2 Another variation is to impose a given length on your story: e.g. 50 or 80 words. Such a restriction will force you to weigh each word very carefully (see *Expanding and contracting*, page 12).

You can start practising by trying to write a very short story, or article, of exactly 45 words, like the following example:

Erreur Three French women who had booked a holiday in Portsmouth, New Hampshire, USA, took a ferry to Portsmouth, Hampshire, Britain. They realised their mistake only when the local cab driver was unable to take them to the Sheraton hotel where they had rooms reserved.

(From *The Economist*, 18 September 1993)

Exchange and discuss your stories afterwards.

Then look again at the story you wrote about the painting in Activity 1. Can you reduce it by exactly twenty words?

3 Do Activity 1 with another painting, imposing your own linguistic rules this time, instead of choosing from the above list. When you have finished, see if the other students can find out what rules you have followed. Then discuss the stylistic effect of your text.

C.7 Exercises in style

The name of this activity is that of a translation of Raymond Queneau's *Exercices de Style*, in which the same incident is related in 99 different ways. Here, you are invited to do something similar.

1 As a class, choose one of the following situations, which will have to be related from the point of view of an outside narrator.

  – In a café. Someone comes in, orders a coffee, drinks it, and leaves without paying.

  – In a stationer's. A woman is returning a fountain-pen which, she claims, does not work. The saleswoman tells her she must have damaged it as it worked before. Both get angry and another customer has to interfere to stop them from fighting.

- In a queue at a ticket counter in a station. Two people, a man and a woman, claim they were there first. Both are in a hurry and give good reasons why their turn should be next.

- In a theatre, just as the performance is about to begin. Two people have been issued a ticket for the same seat. They argue. The people around want them to be silent.

2 Now choose, individually, how to vary the following in your narrative:

- the tone (e.g. amused, detached, outraged, ironic);

- the personality of the narrator (e.g. hesitant, confident, boasting, ashamed);

- the profession of the narrator, which should then appear through the way he or she speaks, the similes used, the comments made (e.g. teacher, lorry-driver, butcher, psychiatrist, MP).

You can now write your own 'variation on the theme'.

Then compare the texts written in your group and discuss the ways in which they differ. Can you guess the personality and profession of the narrators in each case?

3 You can also do the same exercise in a much freer way. Once you have decided as a class on the initial situation, you can choose other aspects or areas for variations. For example, you could choose to vary a linguistic feature such as sentences (short terse ones or long complex ones) or to vary the register (e.g. official, conversational, slang, dialect).

C.8 Evaluation

C.8.1 Blurbs

1 Here are excerpts from reviews of a detective story by P.D. James, *Devices and Desires*. They appear as part of the cover blurb and are, of course, all highly positive.

> "By far the best detective novel to have appeared this year."
> *(Harriet Waugh, Spectator)*

‘Disturbing and challenging, penetrated by acute insight into human torment. The conversation revealing the killer's identity is as brilliant a dissection of moral choice as any I have read.’
(Marcel Berlins, The Times)

‘Her best for years … the characters are vibrant, the writing distinguished, the descriptions of mood and landscape perfect.’
(Graham Lord, Sunday Express)

‘Another magnificent achievement … A compelling human drama that will keep your phone off the hook for days.’
(Kate Saunders, Evening Standard)

‘An elegiac book, rare in murder stories, and should be read by fans not only of death but of life.’
(Candia McWilliam, Observer)

Though the reviewers agree in their praise of *Devices and Desires*, each of them highlights a different aspect of the novel. It is another instance of 'variations on a theme'.

2 1 Think of a book that the whole group knows well. If you cannot think of a book in English, choose one in your language and imagine a translation of it. Each of you should write three or four lines that might be part of the blurb on the cover. You must therefore:

– write these lines as if they were part of a review, its conclusion for example;
– find something positive to say about the book (since the text will appear on the book cover).

C.8

When you have finished, compare the different texts written in your group. Do they all emphasize the same aspect of the book? Are some more laudatory than others? Which of them most make you feel like reading the book?

2 Imagine you are the publisher of the book. You wish to include four or five quotations as part of your blurb. Which would you choose? Remember you want excerpts that:

– make the reader want to buy the book;
– are well written;
– stress different aspects of the book (character, plot, style, etc.).

C.8.2 Reviews

1 Read these two short book reviews from the *Observer* and then answer the
questions.

**Dead Ahead by Ruby Horansky
(Piatkus Crime £12.95)**

Her first homicide case for newly-fledged Detective Nikki Trakos,
desperate to hold her own in a man's
world. A drifter shot in a parking lot at
the squalid end of Brooklyn, an
explosion on a tycoon's yacht (no
corpse recovered), the grim Latino
butler up to something – but what? – in
a sleazy motel, time running out for
Nikki before she has to hand the case
over. Strong on atmosphere and
procedure, some genuine deduction for
a welcome change ... Ruby Horansky
is just about the most impressive
newcomer since Sara Parestky with
whom, substituting New York for
Chicago, she and her lanky intuitive
heroine have much in common.

(From the *Observer*, 5 April 1992)

**The Death and Life of Sylvia Plath
by Ronald Hayman (Minerva £6.99)**

The flood of biographies of Sylvia
Plath is a phenomenon virtually
without parallel since the death of
Byron, and there are plenty more to
come. Hayman's biography has the
advantage of being written without the
constraints of the Plath estate, which
means however there are virtually no
quotations from the poetry, and
Hayman is perceptive and crass in
equal measure. Jacqueline Rose's
study, recently published in paperback
by Virago, remains by far the best
work on the subject to date.

(From the *Observer*, 26 April 1992)

Are these reviews purely positive or do they contain criticisms as well?
Quote passages to justify your opinion.

What devices are used by the critic in the first review to tell readers what
the book is about without revealing the whole plot or the end of the story?

ST CLARE'S

2 Choose a well-known book you have read (even one written some centuries ago) and write a short review of it for the *Observer* in no more than 120 words. Do not mention the title or the author's name.

The table below gives some words and expressions which you may find useful for your review. But the list is far from complete since there are almost endless ways of expressing one's opinion. You could add other expressions to the list as you come across them.

Praise		Criticism
An absorbing	drama	... may irritate some
animated	thriller	a bland film
powerful	documentary	cheap effects
exciting	sitcom	laborious plot
sentimental	series	appalling sets
hilarious	portrayal of ...	conventional story
delightful		poor plot
inventive		inconsistent characters
enjoyable		an unsuccessful attempt to ...
charming		may appeal more to ... than to ...
lively		some readers may regret ...
striking		it seems too ...
bold		the result is too ...
compelling		it lacks ...
convincing		
superb		
fascinating		
exhilarating		
authentic		
meticulous		
comprehensive		
compassionate		
lucid		
shrewd		
sympathetic		

C.8

When you have finished, exchange your review with others in your group and try to identify the books they have reviewed. Do you think the reviews are fair? Do they make accurate and perceptive assessments of the books?

3 Write a short review of a television programme or film which you have recently watched. Do not mention the name of the programme.

Here are two such reviews you can use as models.

Labours of Eve, BBC2

From 60-year-old mothers to sperm banks open all hours, conception is never far out of the news. But what about the lives behind the headlines? *Labours of Eve* aims to uncover the heartaches and traumas behind the medical advances. In a six-part documentary, six women talk about their experiences. Although it smacks of tabloid TV masquerading as serious investigation, this makes compelling viewing. ***

(From *New Woman*, March 1995)

JANE EYRE   (US 1944)

Charlotte Brontë's classic is given a slow-moving but nevertheless powerful rendering in this excellent gothic production by Fox. Orson Welles is menacingly passionate as the irascible Mr. Rochester, and Joan Fontaine is practically perfect as plain Jane. Swirling with atmosphere, this is not the ultimate film of the novel, but pretty good all the same.
Recommended.

Exchange the reviews written in your group and discuss them. Can you recognize the programmes or films reviewed? Are they fair reviews?

C.8

Part *D* Invention

To write is to write is to write is to write
is to write is to write is to write is to write.

(Gertrude Stein)

In the previous parts of this book the activities gradually progressed from fairly controlled writing tasks to much freer ones, while still maintaining a number of constraints (e.g. the imitation of a genre or a writer's style).

The activities in this part are much closer to creative writing. You are encouraged to give free rein to your imagination, with only a few pictures, words or ideas as starting points.

The idea of writing longer texts, or of writing more freely, may seem daunting at first. It shouldn't be. Here are a few tips to avoid the 'fear of the blank page':

1 Do not try to start writing your final story or text immediately. Just think about what you want to say and note down words, expressions or ideas which come to mind.
2 Organize these ideas or words so that you have a clear idea of the structure of your text.
3 Start writing your draft. Do not worry about linguistic accuracy at this point, but try to convey your ideas as clearly as possible.
4 Then read your text over again and start revising it, as you did in 1.1.2 *Editing*.
5 When you feel sure that your text is clear and correct, write the final version.

D

D.1 Chain writing

This is a group activity which is useful for overcoming one's inhibitions when faced with a blank page.

1 Form groups of four to six. Each person writes a title (e.g. 'The Chinese Vase', 'The 25-hour Day', 'A Long Wait', 'In the Year 2005') and a first line on a piece of paper. He or she then passes the piece of paper on to the next student, who adds another line and passes the piece of paper on again. This continues until each student has contributed twice to each text. Contributions should form a consecutive piece of writing: either a story or a poem.

The activity works best if a number of constraints are imposed. You can, for instance, limit the number of words per line: no more than fifteen for a story, no more than six or eight for a poem.

2 Read the whole text aloud and discuss it. What lines were most difficult to follow on from? Why? Are you satisfied with the story or poem as a whole? Can you see ways of improving it?

D.2 Writing about paintings

In this section you are encouraged to write texts related to paintings.

D.2.1 Pages on canvas

Look at the paintings on the next page and decide what each of the two women is reading (e.g. a letter? a message? a poem?) and why she is reacting so strongly.

Write the texts they are reading.

Then exchange and compare the texts written by members of your group.

René Magritte, *The Submissive Reader* 1928 © ADAGP, Paris and DACS, London 1996

William Mulready, *The Sonnet*

D.2.2 Poems about paintings

Many poems describe or take their inspiration from paintings. Such poems mainly originated in the late nineteenth century and early twentieth centuries, when a number of movements closely linked literature and the arts (e.g. the Pre-Raphaelites, the Imagists, the Surrealists). This form of poetry has remained popular ever since.

1 On pages 106–8 are three poems that mention or describe Brueghel's *The Fall of Icarus,* which is reproduced below. Read the poems and answer the questions.

Pieter Brueghel, *The Fall of Icarus*

Landscape with the Fall of Icarus

According to Brueghel
When Icarus fell
it was spring

a farmer was ploughing
his field
the whole pageantry

of the year was
awake tingling
near

the edge of the sea
concerned
with itself

sweating in the sun
that melted
the wings' wax

insignificantly
off the coast
there was

a splash quite unnoticed
this was
Icarus drowning

William Carlos Williams

Musée des Beaux Arts

About suffering they were never wrong,
The Old Masters: how well they understood
Its human position; how it takes place
While someone else is eating or opening a window or just walking dully
along;
How, when the aged are reverently, passionately waiting
For the miraculous birth, there always must be
Children who did not specially want it to happen, skating

On a pond at the edge of the wood:
They never forgot
That even the dreadful martyrdom must run its course
Anyhow in a corner, some untidy spot
Where the dogs go on with their doggy life and the torturer's horse
Scratches its innocent behind on a tree.

In Brueghel's *Icarus*, for instance: how everything turns away
Quite leisurely from the disaster; the ploughman may
Have heard the splash, the forsaken cry,
But for him it was not an important failure; the sun shone
As it had to on the white legs disappearing into the green
Water; and the expensive delicate ship that must have seen
Something amazing, a boy falling out of the sky,
Had somewhere to get to and sailed calmly on.

W. H. Auden

The Bystander

I am the one who looks the other way,
In any painting you may see me stand
Rapt at the sky, a bird, an angel's wing,
While others kneel, present the myrrh, receive
The benediction from the radiant hand.

I hold the horses while the knights dismount
And draw their swords to fight the battle out;
Or else in dim perspective you may see
My distant figure on the mountain road
When in the plains the hosts are put to rout.

I am the silly soul who looks too late,
The dullard dreaming, second from the right.
I hang upon the crowd, but do not mark
(Cap over eyes) the slaughtered Innocents,
Or Icarus, his downward-plunging flight.

D.2

Once in a Garden – back view only there –
How well the painter placed me, stroke on stroke,
Yet scarcely seen among the flowers and grass –
I heard a voice say, 'Eat', and would have turned –
I often wonder who it was that spoke.

Rosemary Dobson

a Whose point of view is expressed in each poem? That of an outside
   narrator? Or that of a character in the painting? If the latter, which one?
b In which of the three poems is *The Fall of Icarus* compared with other
   paintings?
c Which poem mainly focuses on:

   – indifference to pain and disaster
   – secondary characters in paintings
   – the beauty of nature in spite of catastrophe

d Which of the poems best reflects the spirit of the painting, in your
   opinion?
e Which poem do you prefer? Why?

2 Form small groups and look at the painting by Gainsborough on page 86.
   What is its main interest, in your view?

   • its very English landscape
   • what it reveals about the social position of the two characters
   • the contrast between the formal pose of the characters and the natural
     setting
   • the expression on the characters' faces
   • other

   Discuss these points until everyone in your group has chosen an area of
   interest.

D.2

   Then consider individually which point of view could best help to convey this
   idea. For example, if you want to say something about the characters'
   feelings, as shown in their facial expressions, will you describe them as an
   outsider (the point of view Auden and Williams choose in their poems) or
   will you give the interior monologue of one of the two characters (as Dobson
   does)? Discuss these various possibilities, their advantages and drawbacks.

   Now draft a short poem (no more than eight lines) about the painting.

   Exchange your drafts and discuss them. Then see if you can make any
   improvements before writing your final version.

3 Choose one of the paintings reproduced below and write a poem about it. Remember that you can:

- describe the whole painting or only one of its details;
- describe the theme or the technique of the painter;
- describe the painting factually or describe the feelings it evokes;
- describe what *you* see or what one of the characters in the picture sees (the major character? a secondary one?);
- ask yourself questions about what is 'outside the frame': what is unsaid or mysterious in the painting;
- reflect on the painter as much as on the painting: why was such a theme chosen? Why was it treated in such a way?

Paolo Uccello, *St George and the Dragon* (Reproduced by courtesy of the Trustees, The National Gallery, London)

Hopper, Edward. *Second Story Sunlight*. 1960. Oil on canvas. 40 × 50 in. (101.6 × 127 cm). Collection of Whitney Museum of American Art. Purchase, with funds from the Friends of the Whitney Museum of American Art.60.54. Copyright © 1995: Whitney Museum of American Art.

D.2

Then compare your poem with others written in your group about the same painting.

You may now wish to read the following poems inspired by the paintings on page 109.

Not My Best Side

I

Not my best side, I'm afraid.
The artist didn't give me a chance to
Pose properly, and as you can see,
Poor chap, he had this obsession with
Triangles, so he left off two of my
Feet. I didn't comment at the time
(What, after all, are two feet
To a monster?) but afterwards
I was sorry for the bad publicity.
Why, I said to myself, should my conqueror
Be so ostentatiously beardless, and ride
A horse with a deformed neck and square hoofs?
Why should my victim be so
Unattractive as to be inedible,
And why should she have me literally
On a string? I don't mind dying
Ritually, since I always rise again,
But I should have liked a little more blood
To show they were taking me seriously.

II

It's hard for a girl to be sure if
She wants to be rescued. I mean, I quite
Took to the dragon. It's nice to be
Liked, if you know what I mean. He was
So nicely physical, with his claws
And lovely green skin, and that sexy tail,
And the way he looked at me,
He made me feel he was all ready to
Eat me. And any girl enjoys that.
So when this boy turned up, wearing machinery,

D.2

On a really *dangerous* horse, to be honest,
I didn't much fancy him. I mean,
What was he like underneath the hardware?
He might have acne, blackheads or even
Bad breath for all I could tell, but the dragon –
Well, you could see all his equipment
At a glance. Still, What could I do?
The dragon got himself beaten by the boy,
And a girl's got to think of her future.

III
I have diplomas in Dragon
Management and Virgin Reclamation.
My horse is the latest model, with
Automatic transmission and built-in
Obsolescence. My spear is custom-built,
And my prototype armour
Still on the secret list. You can't
Do better than me at the moment.
I'm qualified and equipped to the
Eyebrow. So why be difficult?
Don't you want to be killed and/or rescued
In the most contemporary way? Don't
You want to carry out the roles
That sociology and myth have designed for you?
Don't you realize that, by being choosy,
You are endangering job-prospects
In the spear- and horse-building industries?
What, in any case, does it matter what
You want? You're in my way.

U. A. Fanthorpe

D.2

Hopper at Cape Cod

Sometimes a painting tells us
All we need to know
About our lives, and others'.
This morning I looked
At Hopper's *Second-Story Sunlight*,
Twin gables against thickening trees,
A scrape of shingle, and the light,
All winter soft as cotton wool,
Harsh on the verandah's blistering white.

Preoccupied, austere,
He sits in his dark suit,
Reading the paper. He is impervious
To weather, while she,
Straddling the rail, half-bare,
Unlooses her breasts that loll
With the same sway of boats in swell.

The ice is in his hair
And eyes, for her
This first sun calls
Like a tawny god. She smells
At the resinous, sticky air,
The beating Atlantic. On this springy,
Caressive Cape Cod day,
They seem to pass in mid-stream.
There will be less and less to say.

Alan Ross

D.2

4 Write a fourth part to Ursula Fanthorpe's poem, written from the point of view of the horse or of the spear.

5 Choose a painting and, instead of writing a poem, write a very short story about it.

D.3 From titles to stories

The title of a text is important in that it creates anticipation. But it must not reveal too much about the story, it must not give the game away. This is why it often turns out to have a double meaning, or a meaning which is different from what the reader expects.

Here are the titles of some short stories by well-known writers. Work in pairs or small groups, and discuss the way you understand each of these titles. Use a dictionary if necessary, since some of these titles include set phrases.

Then, working individually, choose one of the titles and write a short synopsis of the corresponding story in no more than 200 words. Do not write the title on your piece of paper. Then exchange your stories and see if you can guess what the other titles might be.

Discuss how effective the relationship between the title and the story is in each case. Did some of you manage to give the title a double meaning?

The Unrest-Cure (Saki)
The Swing of the Pendulum (Katherine Mansfield)
Side Benefits of an Honourable Profession (Doris Lessing)
When Greek Meets Greek (Graham Greene)
The Hypochondriac (Graham Swift)
Stitch in Time (John Wyndham)
The Diamond as big as the Ritz (F. Scott Fitzgerald)
Goodbye and Good Luck (Grace Paley)
The Long Distant Lecture (Elizabeth Jolley)
The Last Laugh (D. H. Lawrence)
A Good Man is Hard to Find (Flannery O'Connor)

D.2

You can also provide titles which the rest of the group could use as starting points for their stories.

D.4 Completing a poem or story

In this exercise you are given the beginning or the end of poems or short stories (sometimes both) and are invited to 'finish' them. You can take each passage in any direction you like, though you have to make sure that there are no inconsistencies between the points of view and narrative techniques used in the short passages you are given and the pieces you add.

D.4.1 Completing a poem

1 Here are two short poems with some lines missing. Can you imagine an end to them?

Celia Celia
When I am sad and weary
When I think all hope has gone
When I walk along High Holborn[1]
....

Adrian Mitchell

Warning

When I am an old woman I shall wear purple
With a red hat which doesn't go, and doesn't suit me,
And I shall spend my pension on brandy and summer gloves
And satin sandals, and say we've no money for butter.
I shall sit down on the pavement when I'm tired
And gobble up samples in shops and press alarm bells
....
....
....
....
....

Jenny Joseph

[1]High Holborn: a street in London.

When you have finished, compare the different endings written in your class. Which ones do you find most moving, interesting or amusing?

(You can then look at the complete poems on page 134 if you wish.)

D.4.2 Completing a story

In the five activities that follow, you are asked to write the beginning, the end or the middle part of a story. Skim through the different texts, choose the one or ones which interest you most and do the activity/activities.

In each case, work on your own, then compare your stories with those of students who have chosen the same activity, and discuss the following points:

- How does each story fit the style of the passage you were given?
- Which plots do you find convincing? Why?
- Can you make any suggestions to improve the other stories?

1 Here is the end of a short story. Imagine what happened earlier and write the beginning of the story, in no more than 200 words.

'The story began badly,' said the smaller of the small girls, 'but it had a beautiful ending.'

'It is the most beautiful story that I ever heard,' said the bigger of the small girls, with immense decision.

'It is the *only* beautiful story I have ever heard,' said Cyril.

A dissentient opinion came from the aunt.

'A most improper story to tell to young children! You have undermined the effect of years of careful teaching.'

'At any rate,' said the bachelor, collecting his belongings preparatory to leaving the carriage, 'I kept them quiet for ten minutes, which was more than you were able to do.'

'Unhappy woman!' he observed to himself as he walked down the platform of Templecombe station; 'for the next six months or so those children will assail her in public with demands for an improper story!'

(From H. H. Munro ('Saki'), *The Story-Teller*)

2 Here is the beginning of a short novel. In no more than 500 words, write a complete story following on from this opening paragraph.

> I did not kill my father, but I sometimes felt I had helped him on his way. And but for the fact that it coincided with a landmark in my own physical growth, his death seemed insignificant compared with what followed. My sisters and I talked about him the week after he died, and Sue certainly cried when the ambulance men tucked him up in a bright-red blanket and carried him away. He was a frail, irascible, obsessive man with yellowish hands and face. I am only including the little story of his death to explain how my sisters and I came to have such a large quantity of cement at our disposal.

(From Ian McEwan, *The Cement Garden*)

3 Here is the beginning and the end of a short story by L. P. Hartley. Imagine what happens in the story and write the middle part of it.

> The circus-manager was worried. Attendances had been falling off and such people as did come – children they were, mostly – sat about listlessly, munching sweets or sucking ices, sometimes talking to each other without so much as looking at the show.

> The circus-manager and his wife stared at each other.
> 'It was the first time he'd done it,' she muttered. 'The first time.' Not knowing what to say to him, whether to praise, blame, scold or sympathize, they waited for him to come back, but he didn't come.
> 'I'll go and see if he's all right,' the circus-manager said. But in two minutes he was back again. 'He's not there,' he said. 'He must have slipped out the other way, the crack-brained fellow!'

(From L.P. Hartley, *A High Dive*)

4 Here is the title, beginning and end of a short story by F. Scott Fitzgerald.
Imagine what happens in the story and write the middle part of it.

Three Hours Between Planes

It was a wild chance but Donald was in the mood, healthy and bored,
with a sense of tiresome duty done. He was now rewarding himself.
Maybe.

When the plane landed he stepped out into a midwestern summer night
and headed for the isolated pueblo airport, conventionalized as an old red
'railway depot'. He did not know whether she was alive, or living in this
town, or what was her present name. With mounting excitement he
looked through the phone book for her father who might be dead too,
somewhere in these twenty years.

On his way to the airport Donald shook his head from side to side. He
was completely himself now but he could not digest the experience. Only
as the plane roared up into the dark sky and its passengers became a
different entity from the corporate world below did he draw a parallel
from the fact of its flight. For five blinding minutes he had lived like a
madman in two worlds at once. He had been a boy of twelve and a man
of thirty-two, indissolubly and helplessly commingled.

Donald had lost a good deal, too, in those hours between the planes –
but since the second half of life is a long process of getting rid of things,
that part of the experience probably didn't matter.

(From F. Scott Fitzgerald)

5 Here are the title and beginning of a short story by W. Somerset Maugham.
Write an ending to the story.

The Escape

I have always been convinced that if a woman once made up her mind to
marry a man nothing but instant flight could save him. ... I have only once
known a man who in such circumstances managed to extricate himself.

His name was Roger Charing. He was no longer young when he fell in love with Ruth Barlow and he had had sufficient experience to make him careful; but Ruth Barlow had a gift (or should I call it a quality?) that renders most men defenceless, and it was this that dispossessed Roger of his commonsense, his prudence, and his worldly wisdom. He went down like a row of ninepins. This was the gift of pathos. Mrs Barlow, for she was twice a widow, had splendid dark eyes and they were the most moving I ever saw; they seemed to be ever on the point of filling with tears; they suggested that the world was too much for her, and you felt that, poor dear, her sufferings had been more than anyone should be asked to bear. If, like Roger Charing, you were a strong, hefty fellow with plenty of money, it was almost inevitable that you should say to yourself: I must stand between the hazards of life and this helpless little thing, oh, how wonderful it would be to take the sadness out of those big and lovely eyes!

When Roger told me that he had at last persuaded her to marry him, I wished him joy.

'I hope you'll be good friends,' he said. 'She's a little afraid of you, you know; she thinks you're callous.'

'Upon my word I don't know why she should think that.'

'You do like her, don't you?'

'Very much.'

'She's had a rotten time, poor dear. I feel so dreadfully sorry for her …'

'Yes,' I said.

I couldn't say less. I knew she was stupid and I thought she was scheming. My own belief was that she was as hard as nails. …

Roger introduced her to his friends. He gave her lovely jewels. He took her here, there and everywhere. Their marriage was announced for the immediate future. Roger was very happy. He was committing a good action and at the same time doing something he had very much a mind to. It is an uncommon situation and it is not surprising if he was a trifle more pleased with himself than was altogether becoming.

Then, on a sudden, he fell out of love. I do not know why. It could hardly have been that he grew tired of her conversation, for she had never had any conversation. Perhaps it was merely that this pathetic look of hers ceased to wring his heart-strings. His eyes were opened and he was once more the shrewd man of the world he had been. He became acutely conscious that Ruth Barlow had made up her mind to marry him and he swore a solemn oath that nothing would induce him to marry Ruth

D.4

Barlow. But he was in a quandary. Now that he was in possession of his senses he saw with clearness the sort of woman he had to deal with and he was aware that, if he asked her to release him, she would (in her appealing way) assess her wounded feelings at an immoderately high figure. Besides, it is always awkward for a man to jilt a woman. People are apt to think he has behaved badly.

Compare the different endings written in your group. Then look at the last few lines of the story:

He sent back his reply by special messenger:
Ruth –
*   Your news shatters me. I shall never get over the blow, but of course your happiness must be my first consideration. I send you herewith seven orders to view; they arrived by this morning's post and I am quite sure you will find among them a house that will exactly suit you.*
Roger

Do these lines lead you to reconsider your own version of what happens at the end?

D.5 Filling the gaps

1 Choose one of the following series of words and write a story in which the words (or the notions they evoke) are used at some point. They can appear in any order you like.

a   bankruptcy   fun   Bahamas   fountain pen   cheating
     appendicitis   copyright   disguise

b   skiing   spy   income tax   Scotland   French cuisine
     thriller   collecting   heart attack

c   bus stop   disappear   bird-watching   scarf   bury
     bank account   competition   steal

When you have finished, compare the different stories written in your group. Then write a similar list of your own and exchange it with your partner. Write a story based on your partner's list and then exchange stories. Has your partner written the story that you expected?

2 Working alone or in groups, write a story linking a sequence of words in the following diagram. You can choose any 'route' you like, provided you start at the top (a hiking holiday) and end at the bottom (a first prize).

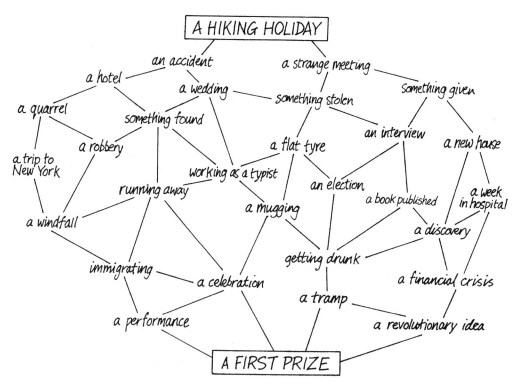

When everyone has finished their stories, some of you can read what you have written to the rest of the class, who can try to trace on the diagram the 'route' followed by each story.

3 The two pictures below are the first and the last of a long series which tells the story of a couple. Imagine what happened in between and tell the story.

Then compare the different stories written in your group.

Sempé, *La Grande Panique*

D.6 Imaginary worlds

There is a long tradition of Utopian writing in English literature. Some works, called 'utopias', imagine and describe ideal countries or communities. Others, called 'dystopias', portray nightmarish societies which point to the dangers in our own world.

1 Here are three excerpts from such works. (You can later look at page 136 to find what books they come from.)

Read the passages and complete the table that follows. Use a dictionary to help you with the more difficult words.

a

> They eat and drink out of vessels of earth, or glass, which make an agreeable appearance though formed of brittle materials: while they make their chamber pots and close-stools[1] of gold and silver; and that not only in their public halls, but in their private houses: of the same metals they likewise make chains and fetters for their slaves; to some of which, as a badge of infamy, they hang an ear-ring of gold, and make others wear a chain or coronet of the same metal; and thus they take care, by all possible means, to render gold and silver of no esteem.

b

> This diversion [rope-dancing] is only practised by those persons who are candidates for great employments, and high favour, at court. They are trained in this art from their youth, and are not always of noble birth, or liberal education. When a great office is vacant, either by death or disgrace (which often happens), five or six of those candidates petition the Emperor to entertain His Majesty and the court with a dance on the rope, and whoever jumps the highest without falling, succeeds in the office. Very often the chief ministers themselves are commanded to show their skill, and to convince the Emperor that they have not lost their faculty.

c

> It's a beautiful thing, the destruction of words. Of course the great wastage is in the verbs and adjectives, but there are hundreds of nouns that can be got rid of as well. It isn't only the synonyms; there are also the antonyms. After all, what justification is there for a word which is simply the opposite of some other word? A word contains its opposite in itself. Take 'good', for instance. If you have a word like good', what need is there for a word like 'bad'? 'Ungood' will do just as well – better, because it's an exact opposite, which the other is not. Or again, if you want a stronger version of 'good', what sense is there in having a whole string of vague useless words like 'excellent' and 'splendid' and all the rest of them? 'Plusgood' covers the meaning; or 'doubleplusgood' if you want something stronger still.'

D.6

[1]Close-stool: a stool with a seat covering a chamber pot; used formerly before the invention of the WC.

	Text (a)	Text (b)	Text (c)
(i) What aspect of society is being described here?			
(ii) What 'original solution' has each of these countries found?			
(iii) What feature of British society is being satirized?			
(iv) Do these texts describe utopias or dystopias?			

Compare and discuss your answers.

2 Think of an aspect of your own or another society which you think is wrong and write a short text about how things work in an imaginary country. You can write about either a utopia or a dystopia.

Then exchange and discuss the texts written in your group.

D.6

KEY

A.1.1 Rewriting

1 Here are possible ways of rewriting the extracts:

  a Bedford firemen today received 28 letters thanking them for their efforts in fighting the fire which destroyed 3 houses last Wednesday night.

  b Bodies in the garden were planted on us says wife.

  c … The board had to be removed before he could be released.

  d The retiring police commissioner has supervised the investigations of all crimes committed in the district for the past twenty years.

  e Now retired, he lives with his wife – a beautiful blonde, who is a San Francisco girl.

  f Man seen yesterday wanted for questioning.

  g … Inflation is blamed.

2 Here are possible ways of rewriting the letters:

  a … I have been ill and in bed for a week, and the doctor doesn't seem to be doing any good. …

  b … Father cannot afford to buy any.

  c Sir, I am sending my marriage certificate as well as the birth certificates of my two children, one of which contains a mistake as you will see.

  d Please send some money as I have fallen into arrears with my landlord.

A.1.2 Editing

1

Alexander was born in 356 BC in Pella, Macedonia, established by his father, Philip II, as the centre of Hellenism. Nurtured on the thoughts of his tutor, Aristotle, he rose to fame as a brilliant military leader. He influenced the course of history, rightfully earning his title as Alexander the Great. In 335 BC he became Military Chief of all the Greeks. By the time of his death in 323 BC he had created an enormous empire, stretching from the Adriatic Sea to the Indias, and from the Caucasian Mountains to Egypt. He spread the Greek spirit far and wide among nations who idolised this great man.

2

Egypt wants Cleopatra's Needle back. The Egyptian embassy claims the ancient obelisk, a London landmark, would be better cared for in Cairo than exposed to the traffic fumes of the Embankment.

'Cleopatra's Needle should be in a museum in Cairo. In London it faces environmental hazards,' said the embassy's cultural councillor Hussein Sayed.

The embassy's call follows a campaign by Egyptian experts who are angry that so much of their heritage is abroad. 'We would like to see the return of important objects to museums in Egypt,' said Professor Abdul Halim Nureldin, Vice-Dean of Cairo University and former director of the government's Antiquities Organisation.

Cleopatra's Needle has had a chequered history. Dating from 1500 BC, it was one of a pair of obelisks carved for Pharaoh Thutmose III and erected at Heliopolis, near modern Cairo. Augustus Caesar moved the two obelisks to Alexandria in 12 BC. Although now known as Cleopatra's Needles, there is no historical basis to the romantic story linking them to the Egyptian queen.

Britain was given one of the obelisks in 1819 by Viceroy Mohammed Ali, an Albanian who ruled Egypt for the Turks. The gift was to thank Lord Nelson for defeating the French and restoring Turkish control.

Cleopatra's Needle had long toppled over and was lying abandoned in the sand. The task of shipping the 186-tonne pillar was daunting and it was not until 1877 that a cylindrical iron vessel was built to transport it to London.

3 Here is a possible way of rewriting the letter with minimal editing:

Dear Mr Richards

It's about Mrs Scott who died. I know all about you and her but I wonder whether Mrs Richards does. I know ALL about it. I hope you believe me, because if you don't I am going to tell her everything. You don't want that and I am not going to tell her if you agree. You are rich and a thousand pounds is nothing to you. If you agree, I will not bother to write again. I keep my promises, believe me. The police don't know anything and I have never mentioned it to anyone. This is what you have to do. Go down to Walton Street in Jericho and turn left into Walton Well Road and then straight on over the little canal bridge and then over the railway bridge. You will come to a parking area where you can't go much further. Turn round and face Port Meadow and you will see a row of willow trees. The fifth from the left has got a big hole in it about five feet from the ground. So put the money there and drive away: I will be watching all the time. I will give you a ring soon, and that will be the only time. I hope you will not try anything funny. Please remember your wife.

4 Here is a possible way of rewriting the letters:

Letter 1

Dear Messrs. Plugg and Gaskett,

I see by your advertisement that you require a junior clerk who is good with figures. You say you would prefer someone who has just left school, so I thought that I might apply. I was third in my class in maths and top in algebra, and I was fairly good at most subjects except English grammar and composition.

I am very interested in motor engineering and would find a job of this kind stimulating.

Yours sincerely,
J. HOOP

Letter 2

Dear Uncle George,

I am writing to ask if you could do me a favour as Dad says you might. The thing is, I have been trying to get a job in an office now that I have left school and have answered twelve adverts in the paper but haven't had any replies, and I think it is probably because I don't know how to write business letters. Dad says that as you are a businessman and better educated than the rest of the family, you could perhaps help me. I would be very grateful as I am at my wits' end and don't want to become a butcher's boy or anything like that.

I hope you are well.
Your affectionate nephew,
JAMES

Letter 4

Dear Mr Hoop,

It seems from your letter that you are just the sort of person we are looking for, though I ought to explain that my little business is not a big concern like the one your uncle works for. But now that we are doing a little more trade we could do with someone to look after the books properly. Most of all, we need someone who can write proper business letters and this seems to be something you are good at. Drop round any time.

Yours sincerely,
SAM BAGGS
C. E. DAVIS

A.1.3 Punctuating

Explanation: a He explained a theory.
              b He explained that the theory was very impressive.

1 a (i)   He has only one nephew.
     (ii) He has several nephews.
  b (i)   Not any MP, but the one who had just been elected.
     (ii) The local MP, or the MP who has already been mentioned.
  c (i)   Those who were reluctant to leave received an invitation.
     (ii) Those who were reluctant were invited to leave.
  d (i)   What is surprising is that she gave the right answers.
     (ii) What is surprising is that she was excited.
  e (i)   Anne and Christine are not his two sisters.
     (ii) Anne and Christine are his two sisters.
  f (i)   All the members were furious.
     (ii) Only the members who had not been warned were furious.
  g (i)   It is the director who had a brilliant idea.
     (ii) It is Brian who had a brilliant idea.
  h (i)   People knew that she would resign.
     (ii) People knew what he thought.

2 Here are the sentences from the original:

  a The gun was among a jumble of textbooks, dog-eared exercise books,
     crumpled paper and a pair of football socks, and for a single frightening
     moment Martin thought it was real.
  b He had come out early, not only to take his son to school – that was
     incidental, a by-product of leaving the house at ten to nine – but to have
     a new pair of windscreen wipers fitted to his car.
  c His credit card would not be needed here to back the cheque, for
     everyone knew him, this was where he had his account; he had already
     caught the eye of one of the cashiers and said good morning.
  d The man, who had the gun in his hand, said in his flat nasal tones,
     'Nothing will happen to you if you do as you're told.'
  e Martin shouted, 'Get back! Call the police! Now! There's been a
     robbery.'

Possible alternatives for (d) and (e) are:

  d The man who had the gun in his hand said, in his flat nasal tones, 'Nothing
     will happen to you if you do as you're told.'
  e Martin shouted, 'Get back! Call the police now! There's been a robbery!'

3 The originals are as follows:

Passage 1

The European Community was a success story, as was evident from the number of applicants waiting to join. In a speech reflecting last Friday's Birmingham summit, the Queen said: 'The British presidency is working to build on that success, developing a community of all 12 member states, which draws on the strength of each, which meets the needs of their people, listens to their anxieties and responds to their wishes – a community which is open to the rest of Europe and to the world.'

Passage 2

At the top of the hill Will pulled to the side and turned off the engine. 'There you are,' he said. Through the windscreen Emmy saw layers of interlocking snow-covered hills receding one after another. ...

'Well?' Will said. He smiled at Emmy, but made no move. She tried to think of something to say, hunting nervously about in her mind, and managed:

'Breughel. ... It's like "The Hunters in the Snow", with all the houses and people taken away.'

Will made no comment. Finally he said: 'Tell me about your parents. You like them, don't you?'

'Yes, I do, really,' she heard herself answer.

'What are they like? Very old family and keeping-up-the-Stockwell-traditions?'

'Oh, no. You've got quite the wrong idea. The Stockwells aren't anything; really.'

'Really? *Nouveau riche?*'

4 The original is as follows:

Half a century after the engraver, letterer and sculptor Eric Gill died, his spirit and philosophy live on through his last pupil, David Kindersley.

This week, apprentices from Kindersley's Cambridge workshop are perched on scaffolding above Euston Road, adding the ring of the hammers and chisels to the whine of London traffic as they cut the words THE BRITISH LIBRARY in enormous Roman capitals from blocks of red Scottish sandstone.

Kindersley, now 77, bearded and with a long, balding head not unlike Gill's, wraps the proceedings in rich wafts of cigar smoke as he talks about his mentor.

He says: 'Gill believed in making things that people wanted. He used to talk about "this art nonsense" and ask, "What's it all for?" Most especially, he was totally at variance with the teaching of art in art schools.' ...

Like Gill, Kindersley insists that his apprentices come to him free of artistic training. He points to the letterers ranged along the scaffolding: 'Cornelia arrived from Holland on a bicycle, she had been a teacher, but felt she needed to make things with her hands. Guy used to be a civil servant. Owen has just left high school in Yukon.'

A.2.2 Contracting

3 a Queens Park, professional male/female, non-smoker, own large room, share house near tube etc.
  b Wimbledon. Immaculate 2-bedroomed house in private mews. Patio/garden, private parking, very close to British Rail/tube. £180 per week.
  c Clapham South. Immaculate 2 double-bedroomed house. Luxury fully furnished kitchen including dishwasher, washing machine. Large bathroom. Sunny garden. £200 per week.

A.3 Completing

1 *Ellison Liddell was a self-made man and inordinately proud of his handiwork.*

Born into a large family of humble parentage, he had soon shaken off his working-class origins and by single-minded deployment of his considerable abilities in the field of electronics, his innovative talent, capacity for hard work and sheer ruthlessness in the removal of all obstacles, he had, in his late forties, acquired very healthy business interests, a large, imposing, exquisitely furnished house, expensive cars, holiday properties overseas and not one financial cloud in his successful sky. Most men in his position would have been content to rest upon their laurels. Not so Ellison.

He had enjoyed accumulating his wealth; now he aspired to two more of life's glittering prizes – an honour of some sort and an heir. The stumbling-block to both these ambitions lay in the person of his wife, Dulcie.

Recently, he had spent much time painstakingly cultivating the 'right' people and, although normally careful with money, had begun giving largely to worthy causes, pretending dismay when the news of his 'secret' generosity was carefully leaked.

Unfortunately, Dulcie did not share his social aspirations, proving, in fact, a distinct embarrassment to them, so, with the ruthless efficiency that characterized all his enterprises, he decided to dispose of her, completely and soon. She was too old, anyway, to provide him with the son he so desired and now that he had met Violette, a lovely, thirty-year-old French woman, widow of a former business competitor, he knew he had found the perfect partner. Wealthy in her own right, she possessed the looks, breeding and business acumen that made her infinitely attractive in his eyes. What a hostess she would make! What a fitting mother of his children! He sensed also, correctly, that she was equally attracted to him, for he had retained his early good looks and was not without a certain facile charm. Only dull, dreary little Dulcie stood between him and the perfect marriage. Dulcie was a drag. Dulcie must go.

2 [Richard Pratt] hesitated, and we waited, watching his face. Everyone, even Mike's wife, was watching him now. I heard the maid put down the dish of vegetables on the sideboard behind me, gently, so as not to disturb the silence.

'Ah!' he cried. 'I have it! Yes, I think I have it!'

For the last time, he sipped the wine. Then, still holding the glass up near his mouth, he turned to Mike and he smiled, a slow, silky smile, and he said, 'You know what this is? This is the little Château Branaire-Ducru.'

Mike sat tight, not moving.

'And the year, 1934.'

We all looked at Mike, waiting for him to turn the bottle around in its basket and show the label. …

'Michael!' his wife called sharply from the other end of the table. 'What's the matter?'

'Keep out of this, Margaret, will you please?'

Richard Pratt was looking at Mike, smiling with his mouth, his eyes small and bright. Mike was not looking at anyone.

'Daddy!' the daughter cried, agonized. 'But, Daddy, you don't mean to say he's guessed it right!'

'Now, stop worrying, my dear,' Mike said. 'There's nothing to worry about.'

I think it was more to get away from his family than anything else that Mike then turned to Richard Pratt and said, 'I'll tell you what, Richard, I think you and I better slip off into the next room and have a little chat.'

'I don't want a little chat,' Pratt said. 'All I want is to see the label on that bottle.'

He knew he was a winner now; he had the bearing, the quiet arrogance of a winner, and I could see that he was prepared to become thoroughly nasty if there was any trouble. 'What are you waiting for?' he said to Mike. 'Go on and turn it round.'

Then this happened: the maid, the tiny, erect figure of the maid in her white-and-black uniform, was standing beside Richard Pratt, holding something out in her hand. 'I believe these are yours, sir,' she said.

Pratt glanced around, saw the pair of thin horn-rimmed spectacles that she held out to him, and for a moment he hesitated. 'Are they? Perhaps they are, I don't know.'

(…) Without thanking her, Pratt took them up and slipped them into his top pocket, behind the white handkerchief.

But the maid didn't go away. She remained standing beside and slightly behind Richard Pratt, and there was something so unusual in her manner and in the way she stood there, small, motionless and erect, that I for one found myself watching her with a sudden apprehension. Her old grey face had a frosty, determined look, the lips were compressed, the little chin was out, and the hands were clasped together tight before her. The curious cap on her head and the flash of white down the front of her uniform made her seem like some tiny, ruffled, white-breasted bird.

'You left them in Mr Schofield's study,' she said. 'On top of the green filing cabinet in his study, sir, when you happened to go in there by yourself before dinner.'

It took a few moments for the full meaning of her words to penetrate, and in the silence that followed I became aware of Mike and how he was slowly drawing himself up in his chair, and the colour coming to his face, and the eyes opening wide, and the curl of the mouth, and the dangerous little patch of whiteness beginning to spread around the area of the nostrils.

'Now, Michael!' his wife said. 'Keep calm now, Michael, dear! Keep calm!'

3　She was about forty-five or fifty years old, and the moment she saw him, she gave him a warm welcoming smile.

'Please come in,' she said pleasantly. She stepped aside, holding the door wide open, and Billy found himself automatically starting forward into the house. The compulsion or, more accurately, the desire to follow after her into that house was extraordinarily strong.

'I saw the notice in the window,' he said, holding himself back.

'Yes, I know.'

'I was wondering about a room.'

'It's all ready for you, my dear,' she said. She had a round pink face and very gentle blue eyes.

'I was on my way to The Bell and Dragon,' Billy told her. 'But the notice in your window just happened to catch my eye.'

'My dear boy,' she said, 'why don't you come in out of the cold?'

'How much do you charge?'

'Five and sixpence a night, including breakfast.'

It was fantastically cheap. It was less than half of what he had been willing to pay.

'If that's too much,' she added, 'then perhaps I can reduce it just a tiny bit. Do you desire an egg for breakfast? Eggs are expensive at the moment. It would be sixpence less without the egg.'

'Five and sixpence is fine,' he answered. 'I should like very much to stay here.'

'I knew you would. Do come in.'

She seemed terribly nice. She looked exactly like the mother of one's best school-friend welcoming one into the house to stay for the Christmas holidays. Billy took off his hat, and stepped over the threshold.

'Just hang it there,' she said, 'and let me help you with your coat.'

There were no other hats or coats in the hall. There were no umbrellas, no walking-sticks – nothing.

'We have it all to ourselves,' she said, smiling at him over her shoulder as she led the way upstairs.

A.4.1 Transforming

2 A possible way of rewriting the instructions is:
Please observe the following rules:
Don't waste water.
Don't use the immersion heater in the master bathroom, the swimming-pool filter or the dishwashing machine at the same time.
Disconnect the refrigerator if you are using a hair-drier.
Consult the instructions found on the walls near the appliances concerned.
Never flush the lavatory next to the small sitting-room more than once every half hour.

B.1.2 Acrostics

a Here are possible answers:

	Stanza 1	*Stanza 2*
Key word	*nonentity*	*endurance*
Similar semantic field	*without achievement*	*surviving*
Opposite semantic field	*fame*	*breaching sorrows*

B.1.2 Advertisements

1 The ad in (a) is obviously based on the expression 'Handle with care'. In (b) there is a pun on the expression 'pressing clothes' (i.e. ironing them). The ad in (c) uses the expression 'on the threshold of' instead of 'about to' since it is about buying a new home. 'Carry you over' also refers to the tradition of the man carrying his bride over the threshold of their new home. In (d) it is the idiomatic expression 'to keep up with the Joneses' which is modified.

B.1.6 Riddles

1 a stairs   b love

Techniques used:
a Indirect description of the object and of its function through metaphors.
b Each of the letters which make up the word is described indirectly by giving examples of other words in which it is or isn't found.

4 Title of Sylvia Plath's poem: 'Mirror'

B.1.7 Tall tales

2

Beginning of the sentences marked by:	End of the sentences marked by:
ordinariness *expectation of a normal story*	*a contrast* *b exaggeration* *c impossibilities*
Examples:	Examples:
The only fish to be caught ... *The only time the sun ever shines ...* *When I started catching cat fish ...*	*a the only rains are dust storms* *b the only way I can whistle is by ringing a bell* *c the pores of my skin are sprouting watercress*

B.3 Retelling a well-known story

1 Here are the plots of the traditional versions of the tales which were originally written by Perrault.

Bluebeard

Bluebeard goes on a journey leaving his new wife the keys of his castle, but forbidding her to enter one room. Curiosity overcomes her and she opens the door to find the bodies of all Bluebeard's former wives. On his return he finds a blood spot on the key which tells him of his wife's disobedience. He is about to cut off her head when her two brothers rush in and kill him.

(From *Brewer's Dictionary of Phrase & Fable, 14th Edition*)

Little Red Riding Hood

Little Red Riding Hood is sent by her mother to take a cake and a pot of butter to her sick grandmother. She loiters on the way, and gets into conversation with a wolf, who learns her errand. He hurries on, eats up the grandmother, takes her place in the bed, and impersonates her when Red Riding Hood arrives, finally devouring the child.

(From P. Harvey (ed.), *The Oxford Companion to English Literature*)

B.4.2 Parodying prose

1

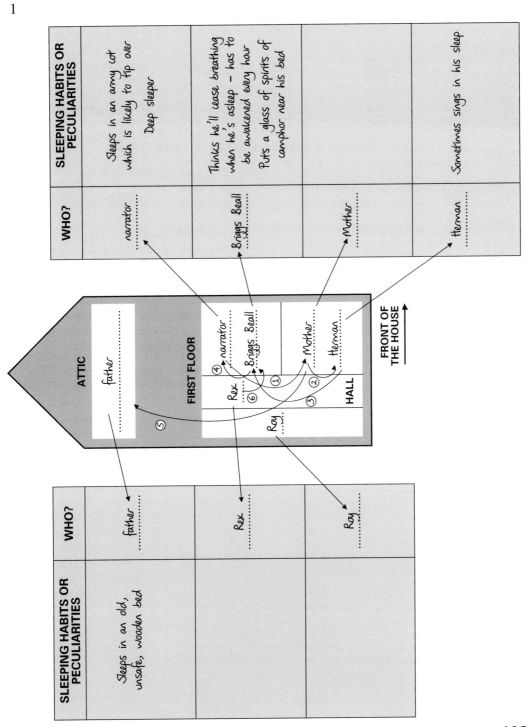

SLEEPING HABITS OR PECULIARITIES	WHO?
Sleeps in an army cot which is likely to tip over. Deep sleeper	narrator
Thinks he'll cease breathing when he's asleep – has to be awakened every hour. Puts a glass of spirits of camphor near his bed	Briggs Beall
	Mother
Sometimes sings in his sleep	Herman

WHO?	SLEEPING HABITS OR PECULIARITIES
father	Sleeps in an old, unsafe, wooden bed
Rex	
Ray	

C.4.2 Turning one genre into another

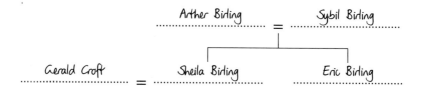

D.4.1 Completing a poem

Lines missing:

'Celia':   I think of you with nothing on.

'Warning'   And run my stick along the public railings
            And make up for the sobriety of my youth.
            I shall go out in my slippers in the rain
            And pick the flowers in other people's gardens
            And learn to spit.

D.6 Imaginary worlds

1 a Thomas More, *Utopia*
     b Jonathan Swift, *Gulliver's Travels*
     c George Orwell, *1984*